After a few short minutes of
came Snow White herself to come talk to Ben.

All of a sudden, a huge smile filled Ben's face and he started laughing hysterically. He was positively transfixed.

Snow White continued to talk to him as Ben very shyly took her hand, and then laughed some more. It was an almost drunken laugh, the laugh you hear from a baby when you play peek-a-boo for too long and they drift into that delirious-happy state. As Snow White talked to him about the ride, and about all of the dwarfs, Ben seemed to be absolutely glowing with joy. A crowd began to gather behind him, and I had to take off my glasses and dry my eyes. I can assure you that I am the manliest of men, and I am positive it was just allergies or perhaps a speck of dust that got in my eye. Whatever it was, it seemed to be spreading to everyone nearby. There was not a dry eye in the house.
   - **From the final night of Snow White's Scary Adventures**

"**Brimming with heart and tragedy overcome**, this is a book that captures the tribulations of parenthood, the magic of Disney World, and the wonderful online communities that allow us to lend aid and comfort to strangers around the world."
Cory Doctorow, *New York Times* best-selling author of *Homeland, Little Brother*, and *Down and Out in the Magic Kingdom*

3500:

An Autistic Boy's Ten-Year Romance with Snow White

By Ron Miles

FIRST EDITION, MARCH 2013

Cover design by Michael Montoure.
www.bookmutant.com

All photos, unless otherwise noted, are © 2013 by Ron Miles.

The photo "Exiting the Ride" taken by Kevin Yee, used by permission.

Benjamin's Lullaby (A.K.A. All Is Well) – Music and lyrics © 2012 by Ron Miles.

"All Is Well" AppleHeart design by Erick Moya
www.moeracreative.com

For permission requests address:
ron@jamesaxler.com

www.shmoolok.com

PRINTED IN THE UNITED STATES OF AMERICA

"The attendant felt nostalgia and kinship. He hoped the bearded man didn't live too far away. If his home was outside practical commuting distance to Dreamworld, the bearded man was going to have to move. The way the attendant had."

from **The Free Lunch** by Spider Robinson

Thank You to the Walt Disney Company for all of the joy you have brought to my family, particularly to my son.

Thank You to my wife Kristine for standing by me and for supporting me throughout this project. I literally could not have done it without you.

Thank You to Riff Millar for being the best of friends, for being a super-ninja packer and moving truck loader, and for driving across America with me.

Thank You to Michael Montoure for your help, guidance and inspiration in turning this book from an idea into a reality.

Thank You to all of the Axlers – Mark Ellis, Rik Hoskin, Cathy Joyce, Victor Milan, Alan Philipson, Chuck Rogers, and Douglas Wojtowicz. Each of you has inspired me over the past fifteen years; without you I would have never even dreamed of attempting this project.

Thank You to Matthew Upchurch, Kristi Jones, David Hansen, Scott Ahlsmith, Amelia Ross, and all of Virtuoso for being the best company for which I could ever imagine working.

Most of all, Thank You to my son Benjamin. In the words of Jonathan Coulton, "*You ruined everything, in the nicest way.*"

Author's Note

Before I begin telling this story, I need to clarify a few things right from the start.

First of all, if you picked up this book expecting to read a story about how a theme park attraction miraculously cured an autistic boy then you are going to be sadly disappointed. Although Ben's time spent with Snow White's Scary Adventures had a dramatic and positive effect on him, at nineteen years old he still remains a profoundly disabled individual. He continues to require full-time supervision and is thus far completely incapable of living independently. In fact, that is precisely why I have written this book — sharing his story is Ben's best opportunity to support himself and provide some measure of security, and every single penny of any revenue this book generates will go directly into his Special Needs Trust to provide for his long term care.

Next, although this is Ben's story, it is by necessity told from my perspective. It is an unfortunate reality that a large percentage of marriages with special needs children end in divorce; sadly our marriage was no different. Please do not mistake the minimal appearance of Ben's maternal side of the family in this book to mean they are not involved in his life. Quite the opposite is true: Ben is blessed with a very caring mother who is, in fact, his legal Guardian Advocate now that he is an adult and who has been his primary caregiver since the day he was born. In every aspect of his life she has been intimately and lovingly involved. That includes his entire experience with Disney and Snow White. Benjamin also has two maternal aunts and a maternal grandmother and grandfather, all of whom play significant ongoing roles in his life.

I am very much aware of the fluid nature of memory. Much of this book has been constructed based on contemporaneous journal entries or blog posts I wrote at the time these things happened, but a significant part of the book is based purely on my memories of past events. Some passages are stories that I have told verbally so many times over the years that I honestly can't say whether I am describing a memory of an actual event or a memory of a memory of a retelling of that event. The most I can say is that everything in this book is what I remember and believe to be the truth. But if, say, Ben's mother were to write a book about the same things, then I have no doubt the telling would be very different. The best I can do is to be as honest with my memories as possible and hope that the truth remains, well, *true*.

Finally, I must give credit to the uniformly excellent teachers, therapists, and administrators at Princeton House Charter School and Access Charter School where Ben has attended for the past seven years. While it was Walt Disney World and Snow White's Scary Adventures that provided the fulcrum to move Ben's world, to a very large degree it has been the dedicated educators at PHCS and ACS who have given us the lever to take advantage of that opportunity.

The simple truth is that Ben has always been surrounded by people who love him and support him. I am grateful for every single one of them.

Thank you so much, from the bottom of my heart.

Chapter 1

Christmas Day, 1993

Benjamin was a genuine Christmas gift, albeit one that took nearly forty hours to unwrap. His mother Sara and I were young newlyweds – we met in the fall of 1992, fell madly in love, were married only a few months later, and now here we were about to celebrate the end of 1993 by bringing a new child into our young family.

We spent Christmas Eve with my mother (my parents divorced when I was very young, my father lived a thousand miles away), and then, Christmas Day with Sara's family at her parents' home. The normal helping of Christmas Cheer was amplified by everyone's anticipation of when the baby would arrive. We'd had a few false starts in the previous week, and frankly Sara was ready to be *done* with being pregnant. She was happy but exhausted, and after a full day of holiday celebration we finally made our way back to our tiny apartment in the small farming town of Burlington, Washington. An already-packed bag for the hospital waited by the door. Our family members were all awaiting the call that labor had begun. Sara and I were both anxious with anticipation.

Sure enough, at about 7pm on Christmas Day, Sara stumbled into the living room and declared, "It's time!"

I made two quick phone calls as Sara prepared to go, letting our respective parents know that we were leaving for the hospital and that I would call them with more info after we had seen the doctor. With that, we were off.

This was no false alarm. Sara's water had broken and there was no question that we were going to have a baby very soon. There was an initial flurry of activity as we were admitted to the hospital and placed into a room, but by 9pm things had calmed down considerably. The doctor assured us that nothing much was likely to happen overnight and that we should try to get some rest. The twenty-sixth of December would be the Big Day! I dutifully informed our family where things stood, telling them not to bother coming to the hospital until tomorrow, and then tried to help my wife get the sleep she needed. Christmas came to a close with her sleeping in her hospital bed and me napping on the couch nearby.

The next day was a long and brutal one. I say brutal – it was long and emotionally draining for me, I can only imagine how physically and emotionally punishing it was for Sara. By morning there was still no real progress. The contractions continued to be ages apart and did not seem to be accelerating. Throughout the day family members arrived to provide emotional support. The room filled with doctors and nurses and everyone was focused on Sara. The monitors showed the baby was still healthy, but Sara's body just wasn't cooperating. A Pitosen drip was started to help speed up the labor. Still the baby seemed no closer to being born. Sara had contraction after contraction, in heavy labor but to no apparent end. She was in agony, she was exhausted, and she just wanted it to be *over*. By evening it was clear that the twenty-sixth was not the Big Day after all. I sent the family away to give Sara a little space, a little peace and quiet. The doctor assured us that everything was just fine, the baby was perfectly healthy, and to just hang in there. Neither of us got much sleep that night.

Hour after hour went by, with nurses buzzing in and out of the room at regular intervals to take vital signs on both the mother and the unborn child. Finally, *finally*, at around 7am the next morning the doctor declared that the delivery would have to be done via c-section. As Sara was prepped for surgery I made a few quick phone calls to family to let them know what was happening. I was then given scrubs and walked through properly sanitizing myself so that I could be present during the surgery. A few minutes later I was taken into the delivery room.

Sara lay there on the surgical table in a bright white room filled with scary medical equipment and glaring lights. I was seated by her head holding her hand to reassure her. A curtain was draped across her body to prevent us from seeing the actual surgical incisions. I vividly remember at one point glancing to one side where there was a glass-front cabinet that stored sterile utensils. The pristinely-shined glass acted like a perfect mirror, and I could see the surgeon peeling back my wife's stomach. Decades later it is an image still burned into my retinas. I quickly blanched and turned back to focus on her face to reassure her that everything was just fine. Moments later a baby's cry filled the room, and then the nurse was there handing us our newborn son. After 38 hours of labor, our beautiful baby boy had finally entered the world.

The next six months passed exactly as you would imagine, with diapers and bottles and many a sleep-deprived night. Aside from the fact that he never, ever slept for more than three hours at a stretch, Ben was a normal happy infant and we were a normal, happy-but-exhausted family. Unfortunately, it was in the summer of 1994 that the world began to collapse around us.

Since leaving college I had worked in restaurant and retail management. I started out as a pizza delivery driver, worked my way up to assistant manager, then made a lateral jump to being an assistant manager at a music store. By the time Ben was born I had been the general manager at two different locations of a popular music chain, and my career seemed bright.

Then one day, when Ben was barely six months old, I was unceremoniously fired from my job. My till had come up short by more than $20 on two separate occasions, which led Loss Prevention to suspect that I was a thief. I categorically was not, but my protests and proclamations of innocence fell on deaf ears. One morning out of the blue and without warning the district manager walked into the store, took me in the back, and fired me. To this day I believe that the real reason it happened was because I was the only manager in the district with a child, and my boss simply didn't want to deal with managers who had family obligations. Maybe I was just a bad manager and didn't realize it, who knows? In any case, I had to go home that day and tell my wife that I had no job and no way to put food on the table for my family. It was easily the worst day I had ever experienced in my life to that point. It was also the first crack in the dam of our marriage.

Three months later I was still under-employed (who is going to hire a guy who was fired for theft?) and we were subsisting on food stamps and whatever crumbs we could generate through part-time jobs. We began to be concerned about Ben's development. At nine months he was lagging behind on some of the standard metrics. Although his physical development was normal, he was not displaying the kind of cognitive and sensory skills that are expected by that age. When we expressed our concerns at the regular nine-month checkup, Ben's pediatrician assured us that while Ben was certainly on the low end of the bell curve in many areas, it wasn't that unusual and that every child is unique and progresses at their own rate.

Another three months passed, and I was struck my next personal blow: my father was diagnosed with colon cancer. Despite the initial surgery to remove the cancerous tissue, his long term prognosis was grim. I was able to visit him a few times while he was in town to see his old doctor, but then he returned to his home in Arizona where my only real contact was over the phone.

At about the same time, Ben had his twelve-month checkup, and he showed no significant improvement over his nine-month exam. By now the pediatrician was genuinely concerned and referred us to specialists for additional testing.

At fourteen months, Ben finally received his initial diagnosis of Pervasive Developmental Delays – Not Otherwise Specified (PDD-NOS). That diagnosis would later be upgraded to Autism.

As I sat in that doctor's office and heard the word "autism", my entire body went numb. I had heard of autism but had never to my knowledge directly interacted with an autistic person or their family. My entire frame of reference was films like *The Boy Who Could Fly* or *Rain Man*. I didn't even know what, exactly, autism was.

As we soon discovered, autism is a neurodevelopmental disorder in which, for some reason, the brain does not build the same kind of neural connections that happen in a "normal" brain. This affects how the brain processes information by altering the way that nerve cells and their synapses connect and organize. The result is a person with impaired social interaction skills and with significant sensory integration issues.

Autism is also referred to as a "spectrum disorder", meaning that the severity of symptoms exists on a curve. A high functioning autistic might be able to function fully independently as an adult, while still having difficulty managing social interactions. A low functioning autistic would likely never be able to function independently and would require 24-hour supervision for their entire life. At that point we did not know where on the spectrum Ben would fall, but our doctors told us that early intervention could dramatically improve the outcome.

We began speech and physical therapy right away, but our family was devastated. Our beautiful little boy couldn't talk, wouldn't make eye contact, and was frequently inconsolable. We saw our peers raising happy, healthy children while we were locked in a constant struggle to simply get through the day. Ben still wasn't sleeping with any regularity, and when he was awake he was like the Energizer Bunny – just going, and going, and going … It simply never ended and a full night's sleep was an exceedingly rare treat. I began to sink into depression and the cracks in our marriage grew. It was a matter of "too much, too soon" for a relationship that had not had enough time to build any real foundation.

By the summer of 1995 there was at least one ray of light. After more than a year of working part-time minimum wage jobs to scrape by, I was finally hired at a real full-time job working tech support for the launch of Windows 95. In fact, in one of the last conversations I ever had with my father, he told me me how proud he was that I now had a real job with real potential for a career. Sara, Ben and I did manage to fly down to Arizona to visit my father that summer for what I was sure would be the last time I would ever see him. It was a good visit and Ben handled the trip fairly well (or at least as well as you could expect from an 18-month-old child).

Just two months later I received the phone call I had been dreading. My father was dead. I fell into a deep depression, and I am sure I was both a bad husband and a bad father during that time. No abuse and no fighting, I simply checked out from the world and sleepwalked through each day. Get up, go to work, answer support calls for eight hours, go home, and go to bed. This was the final blow to our marriage, albeit a very slow and drawn out one. It would take over a year to finalize, but our marriage was over.

Despite the failure of our marriage, Sara and I did go on to build a very successful parenting relationship. Whatever other disagreements we might have had, we virtually always agreed upon what was important for Ben. Although we had a standard court-ordered parenting plan that said something like "one weekend per month, two weeks in the summer", in reality we fell into a rhythm of Ben being with his mom during the week and with me on the weekends.

By the time Ben was old enough to begin school Sara and I were both living in Seattle. I had moved from working telephone technical support to becoming a software developer just as the initial internet Dot Com Boom was heating up. Sara attended the University of Washington and ultimately earned her Master's degree as an English teacher. Ben attended Alternative Elementary 2 (AE2), a special environment created by the Seattle Public School District designed specifically for autistic children. On mornings when Sara had to leave for school (or, in later years, for work) before Ben's school bus arrived, I would drive across town to her apartment and get Ben ready for his day. After putting him on the bus I would carry on to my own job. I saw Ben almost every single day at one point or another, and our family thrived despite (or perhaps because of) the divorce. Although Ben was completely non-verbal, he was happy and affectionate, and it was clear that he felt completely loved and supported despite his fractured household.

It was during this time period that his love for Disney began to emerge.

Chapter 2

The 1990s

When Ben was perhaps five years old, his maternal grandmother gave him a large plush Sorcerer Mickey Mouse doll from the movie *Fantasia*, and he absolutely adored it. He carried it with him *everywhere*. Around the house all day, to bed at night, in the car when out running errands, Ben and Sorcerer Mickey were inseparable. When he went to school, Sorcerer Mickey was there in his backpack to be used as a reinforcer for positive behavior. Although Ben would still not make direct eye contact with anyone for more than a split second, in Sorcerer Mickey he seemed to have found a best friend.

Like pretty much any kid his age, Ben liked to watch video tapes. Unlike most kids his age, he had no interest whatsoever in watching television. Broadcast programming held little or no attraction for him because he couldn't control it. You see, he didn't just put in a video tape and watch it. No, he would put in a tape, fast forward it to a particular moment, play it for a few seconds, and then rewind it back to the same point and play it again. The moments he fixated on were all sound-oriented, either something like a whistle or bang or else a particular piece of dialog. The only tapes he was interested in were Disney videos, and the only exceptions he made to that rule were *The Land Before Time* (created by Don

Bluth, an ex-Disney animator) and for some odd reason, *American Tail 2: Fievel Goes West*.

When traveling between households he would bring tote bags filled with his Disney video tapes, and then at my house he also had access to a Laserdisc player, the failed precursor to DVDs. The disc that he loved most was *Fantasia*. He would play "The Sorcerer's Apprentice" on an endless loop.

Ben quickly learned how to manipulate the controls of the VCR, and this soon became a huge problem. All of the rapid fast forward, play, rewind, play, rewind, again and again in the same spot wreaked havoc with the video tapes. It was a depressingly regular occurrence for me to delicately extract a tape that had become jammed up in the player. I learned how to disassemble a VCR in order to extract a particularly tangled up video tape, and I learned how to take apart and reassemble the video tapes themselves when the roll became tangled inside the cartridge. Since all of the constant back and forth would also rapidly gum up the tape heads, another talent I acquired was how to open up a VCR and clean all of the tape heads and mechanisms when a simple head cleaner would not do the trick.

In an effort to minimize his abuse of the video tapes, I took to performing delicate surgery on all of the VCRs we owned. I would open up the case and then physically remove the circuit board behind the buttons on the front panel so that the VCR could only be operated by remote control. Ben's response? Find the remote, regardless of where it was hidden. If he was left alone in the room for three minutes, the room would become a disaster scene that looked like it had been ransacked by police searching for illicit drugs.

One time his mom tried putting the VCR and remotes inside a television cabinet and placing a child-proof lock on the front of the cabinet doors. This seemed to work for a few days, until one morning she came downstairs after getting ready for work only to find the cabinet in ruins. That was one of the days when I came to her place to get Ben ready for school, and she met me at the door glowering and simply said, "Come look and see what your son has done." I walked into that living room to find Ben sitting happily on the floor watching a Disney tape, surrounding by the shattered kindling of the cabinet door lying all around him. He had literally torn the door off of its hinges and ripped it to pieces in order to get at the VCR and watch a Sing-a-long video of *The Little Mermaid*. He was giggling with delight, holding the remote and repeatedly listening to a single phrase from "Under the Sea" in a room that looked like a bomb had gone off.

Time went by. He grew older but still did not speak. Oh, he vocalized endlessly – a nonstop barrage of babbling, screeching, honking noises – but no actual words. His first language actually turned out to be rudimentary sign language. He learned to sign "I want", "please", and "thank you", and began learning a few other words to fill in the blank. The quickest phrase he learned to sign was "I want candy, please!" I was so thrilled the first time he used that in a store that I bought him a big bag of jelly beans right then and there.

Jelly beans aside, his diet in general had become an increasing concern. The only thing he would drink was red Gatorade, and then only from a very specific kind of Tupperware sippy cup. As for food, he steadfastly refused to eat anything that wasn't round. Grapes. Rice cakes. Hot dogs cut into round discs. If it wasn't round, or if it required utensils, he simply refused to eat it. No amount of starvation or withholding would overcome his anxiety; he absolutely would not eat anything new or different no matter what we tried. Fortunately he would eat the rice cakes with peanut butter smeared on them, and so I think from the age of three until ten almost all of his protein came from a jar of JIF.

His sleeping patterns remained equally obstinate. He would run like a machine all day long and well into the night. Bedtime was a daily disaster. It was not unusual for him to be wide awake until two or three in the morning only to wake up again before sunrise. It did not seem to be anxiety driven but rather like he simply could not turn off his brain for more than three or four hours at a stretch. When he stayed the night with me our bedtime routine consisted of me laying down with him in his bed, making sure there were no other distractions (either audio or visual), and simply holding him until he finally fell asleep and I could tiptoe out of the room. Most days with him I was sleep deprived. If he slept for four hours, that meant I only slept for maybe three. Oftentimes he would seem to fall asleep, only to reawaken a few minutes later to jump out of bed and start turning on every light in the house. Many a night felt like a running battle that culminated with him sitting wide awake and joyfully giggling in a dark room while I banged my head against the wall in frustration and begged for relief.

Still in all, despite all the challenges that having an autistic child presented, life was good. On the whole, he was a very happy and affectionate boy; he was just exhausting to care for. Every day we looked for the little triumphs and hoped for the big breakthroughs.

One huge breakthrough was the summer he taught himself how to swim. I wish I could say that I or his mother taught him through a combination of hard work and determination, but of course with Ben it was something much stranger than that.

The apartment complex where I lived had a swimming pool that was generally only open for a few months during the summer. The weather in the Pacific Northwest is only nice enough and warm enough to swim outdoors for perhaps three months out of the year. The rest of the year is spent under constant gray, overcast skies with temperatures that may not be brutally cold but are certainly not warm enough to even consider putting on a swimsuit. But when those summer months roll around and the sun peeks out for a few hours, just look out – people are going to hit the pool at every opportunity. (No sane person hits the beach for swimming in the Pacific Northwest. The beaches are beautiful, and I have spent a great many days on them. That being said, the beaches are drab and rocky and the waters of Puget Sound are perpetually chilly year-round.)

So one summer, I think it was in 2000, I began taking Ben down to the apartment pool often during the weekends. He enjoyed going, but he would never actually get in the water. He just walked around the pool staring intently at the other kids as they swam around having fun. At most, Ben would sit on the edge of the pool and dangle his feet in the water. I tried easing him into the pool a few times, but he would panic and flail so much that I was afraid he would hurt himself. Even so, he kept asking to go to the pool and so all summer long I would put him in a swimsuit, slather him up with sunscreen, grab a book to read, and then go hang out at the pool for a few hours and watch Ben watch the other kids. For the most part the other children at the pool were kind to

Ben and largely ignored him when he failed to respond to their invitations for him to join in whatever games they were playing. Occasionally I would need to explain autism to a curious child, and over time the regulars at the pool just accepted Ben as a spectator and left him to his own devices.

As the summer began to wane in the last weeks of August, the pool grew less crowded. Out of the blue Ben started stepping into the pool. At first he would only get in up to his waist. Then he began to inch further and further towards the deeper water, all the while splashing and laughing merrily. Over the course of two weeks he reached the point where he would go right up to the drop-off where the water suddenly went from five feet deep to nine feet deep. Ben didn't want me anywhere near him. Since he pushed me away whenever I got in and came towards him, I sat anxiously on the edge of the pool watching him with a heady mixture of pride and pure terror.

Then one afternoon he deliberately ducked his head underwater. At first it was a very quick thing, just under and back up, but then he began to stay under for longer and longer stretches of time. By this point he had gotten comfortable with swimming along the water's surface. Now he began swimming underwater with absolute confidence. He never wore swim goggles or a nose plug, and he never pinched his nostrils closed to hold his breath underwater; he would simply sink under the surface and then kick powerfully with his legs while swinging his arms to maneuver. I was so staggered to witness this that I went and bought a disposable waterproof camera so that I could try to see what he was actually doing while submerged. I took an entire roll of film, doing the best I could to point the camera in his general direction without actually being able to frame the shots. If I had been astounded by watching him teach himself how to swim, I was completely gobsmacked when I saw those photos. There he was, swimming like a fish, with his eyes wide open and a huge grin on his face. Without ever being taught, he was clearly slow-breathing underwater. He was as happy as could be, and I was one seriously proud papa.

One thing I know about autistic kids is that they tend to have a lot of sensory integration issues. I think for him, swimming has the dual positives of both literally drowning out the noise of the world around him and also providing a lot of the deep pressure sensory feedback that he craves. Swimming was the most joyous thing Ben had ever discovered, and I still have the collage of those photos framed and sitting on my bookshelf.

Swimming

Ben's first big vocal breakthrough was thanks to his love of Disney music. I would sing to him constantly, mostly Disney songs from his favorite movies. Driving in the car, sitting in our living room, out shopping or getting a haircut, I would sing a regular litany of Disney tunes. His favorite was "The Bare Necessities". I would look him right in the eyes and say, in my best Baloo voice, "It's like this Little Britches: all ya gotta do is..." and then he would clap happily as I started singing, "...look for the bare necessities, the simple bare necessities..."

We were out one day, I forget where – maybe at the local shopping mall – and we were sitting next to each other on a bench while I sang, "Look for the..."

and for some reason I hesitated for a moment. Out of the blue Ben said, "prsch."

It was completely different than any of his regular vocalizations, spoken very specifically if somewhat garbled. Was he trying to finish the phrase and say 'bear'? I didn't want to believe it, I had never in the past seven years heard him attempt to speak an actual word, but there it was. I tried not to react. I didn't want to scare or intimidate him. I just continued on with the song. "…necessities, the simple…"

"Bersch!"

"…necessities, forget about your worries and your…"

"Strph!!"

Oh my God, he was actually talking! Maybe I was the only person on the planet who knew what he was saying, but it was very clear to me that he was trying to fill in the words wherever I paused. I don't think I had ever been happier in my life, and Ben was just beside himself with joy that he was actually interacting with me in a genuine give-and-take manner. I spent the rest of the day singing songs to him, deliberately leaving words out, and reveling in him actually speaking recognizable words. Most parents get to hear their babies speak their first words somewhere around their first birthday, but for us it took a half dozen extra years. Thanks to Disney, my boy was finally starting to talk.

Chapter 3

Spring, 2002

The 90s came and went, and along with them the Dot Com Boom turned into the Dot Com Bust. In the six years since our separation and subsequent divorce, Sara was in the final months of completing her Master's degree while I continued to advance in my career as a software developer. At eight years old Ben was still essentially non-verbal, although he had a few stock spoken phrases he would use. No amount of potty training had achieved any results, and so Ben was still wearing pull-up diapers. He seemed physically very healthy, and his regular physical checkups reflected as such, despite the fact that his diet had essentially degenerated to pretty much just red Gatorade and French fries. I credit my Irish ancestry and the nutritional power of the potato for his survival. Any medications he took either had to come in a liquid form, or else be ground up into powder and dissolved into his juice.

He was on, I think, the third incarnation of the Sorcerer Mickey plush doll, and still carried it with him everywhere. He also carried with him a portable CD player and a booklet holding two dozen Disney CDs wherever he went. He wore a pair of massive full-ear headphones that would drown out the world around him if he became overwhelmed or over stimulated, which was pretty much always.

Unlike me, Sara had grown up in South Florida and her childhood included regular trips to Walt Disney World. I had never been there, but I had been to Disneyland in California a few times and had some happy memories from my visits. We both had dreams of taking our child on his first trip to a Disney park, and we decided that maybe it was time to try. Although Disneyland was closer, we figured if we were going to spend two days traveling on a plane with Ben we may as well go all the way to Florida; in for a penny, in for a pound. It's a very odd thing, to plan a weeklong vacation with your ex-spouse, but ultimately we decided to give it a try for Ben's sake. And so it was that we made our first, fateful trip to Orlando in March of 2002. At the time we expected it to be a simple vacation. We could never have imagined just how drastically it would change our lives.

Because Ben loved Fantasia so much, we considered booking rooms at the All Star Movies resort at Walt Disney World. The hotel features a Fantasia-themed building complete with giant enchanted brooms carrying buckets of water, as well as a Sorcerer's Apprentice themed swimming pool. After talking about it, however, we decided to book rooms next door at the All Star Music resort instead because we were afraid that Ben would get so excited by the giant Fantasia brooms that he would never go to sleep. We figured if we stayed in the resort right next door then the price would be the same (the All

Stars are the Disney "budget" resorts), and we could still walk Ben over to see the Fantasia pool at some point pretty easily. With our lodgings reserved (a pair of adjoining rooms with a pass-thru door), all we had left to do was to wait and anticipate.

There was a particular commercial that was running at the time, and which was featured on the Lion King video tape. I remember it because, well, Ben played it a *lot*. I don't know what it was about the ad that he liked, I really don't think he understood the actual content of the ad, but it was perfectly apropos. It featured a boy, maybe six or seven years old, explaining to his younger brother all the cool things about Walt Disney World as he packs a suitcase. The punch line of the commercial is when the boy sits down next to his brother on top of the fully packed suitcase and says, "We'll be leaving in about… three weeks."

That's pretty much how we felt, counting down the days to the trip. We were anxious about how Ben would do flying on a plane. We were also worried whether Ben would enjoy the theme parks or if he would be too overwhelmed. We were very excited to give him the opportunity to experience Disney up close. Soon enough the day arrived and we made our way to the airport.

Anyone living in the United States may recall that air travel was particularly difficult in the spring of

2002. The wounds of 9/11 were still very fresh and raw, and airport security was absolutely insane. We had checked our suitcases, but we still had several carry-on bags filled with items to entertain and distract Ben during the flight, plus all the supplies you need when going anywhere with a non-potty trained child. Although Ben was eight years old, he was in many respects like an infant. We needed a fully-stocked diaper bag with enough supplies to potentially last up to twelve hours in case flights were delayed or connections were missed. So there we were, working our way through airport security fully laden down with bags, trying to keep Ben calm and contained in a very loud and chaotic space. The potential for Ben getting spooked and running off was very high, so we were watching him like hawks. Naturally, we were selected by security for additional screening.

What the airport security guy wanted was for each of the three of us to go to a different table, each five or ten feet apart, and wait patiently while screeners searched through our bags. I tried to quietly explain to security agent how that just wasn't possible, and he cut me off immediately and again directed us to go to the three separate tables.

"Look," I pleaded, "I'm not trying to be difficult. Our son is autistic. He doesn't understand what you are asking him to do. If he is not holding either my hand or his mother's hand, he may very well run off and hide."

Finally the security agent took another look at Ben, and recognized that this was not a normal kid. Ben was allowed to stay with his mother, while I was directed to a separate table. Eventually the security guards were satisfied that we were not, in fact, terrorists, and we were allowed to proceed to our plane.

The flights themselves seemed very long and even the connection between flights at the mid-point was challenging. Ben was a handful pretty much the entire way. Flying is difficult for any child but is even more so for a kid like Ben who just doesn't understand what is happening. His normal routine was gone, and he had no comprehension of where we were going or why he had to sit in those airplane seats for so long. We did our best to keep him calm, and we spent a fair amount of time apologizing to the passengers around us.

We got into Orlando International Airport well after dark, and then it took close to two hours to get our bags, get a shuttle to the hotel, and get checked in. The All Star Resorts are absolutely enormous. After entering through a front building that contains the check-in desk as well as a gift shop and giant food court, the main courtyard appears where guests are confronted with a giant, themed swimming pool. In

the case of the All Star Music resort, the pool is
shaped like an enormous guitar. Flanking the pool are
sets of buildings, each structure a three story T-
shaped block that is decorated with a particular
theme. The pair of buildings on either side of the
guitar pool are Calypso themed, with giant hundred-
foot-tall maracas on the façade. Walking towards the
back of the complex, past the main pool, the next pair
of buildings has a Jazz music theme. Farther still is
another courtyard with a second, slightly smaller pool
shaped like a piano. To one side is a pair of Rock 'n
Roll buildings, to the other is a pair dressed up for
Broadway, and in the back is one final pair featuring
Country music with giant cowboy boots. Each of the
All Star resorts contains ten of these buildings and
boasts nearly two thousand guest rooms. With three
All Star resorts lined up in a row on the south edge of
the Walt Disney World property, that adds up to
almost six thousand dramatically-themed hotel rooms
along one small stretch of land.

It being the middle of March and with spring
break going on, the resorts were a buzzing hive of
activity well into the night. We were booked into the
Rock section, which, unknown to us before we got
there, was about as far away from the front desk as
possible. We made the trek out to our rooms,
discovered some kind of problem (I don't remember
what any more), and I had to walk all the way back
up to the front desk to sort it out. Whatever the minor
issue was, Guest Services got it fixed promptly and

then I made my third journey across the hotel grounds back to the land of Rock and Roll.

I arrived to find Ben was completely keyed up, both because of being cooped up so long on the two flights and also because with the time change it felt three hours earlier. He was nowhere near ready for bed. Sara had opened the adjoining door between the rooms while she unpacked so that Ben could go back and forth between my room and theirs to explore the space. He particularly enjoyed the bathroom for some reason and sat cross-legged on the tile floor for a while listening to his headphones. Sara and I both freshened up a bit and then decided to go back to the food court to get something to eat. Ben loved the dining facility where he wolfed down a plate of French fries. The combination of all the walking, a full belly, and a little nudge from his medications finally helped to wear Ben down. When we made it back to our rooms Ben fell asleep in the bed next to Sara while I collapsed into my own bed on the other side of the wall.

Ben didn't know it yet, but tomorrow was going to be a Very Big Day.

For our vacation we had four touring days with a travel day on either side. Our plan was to spend the first and last touring days at the Magic Kingdom, spend the second day at Epcot, and divide the third day between Animal Kingdom in the morning and the Disney MGM Studios (since renamed the "Disney Hollywood Studios") for the remainder of the day. If needed we could return to the hotel for a break from the crowded theme parks, perhaps for a nap or a dip in the pool. In a worst-case meltdown scenario we could simply retreat to our rooms and ride it out. We really had no idea which way it would go, whether Ben would love the experience or be driven insane by all the stimulation. It was a total crap shoot, so that next morning we boarded a shuttle bus to the Magic Kingdom prepared for any kind of emergency and hoping for the best.

For his part, Ben just seemed mostly confused. He had no concept of where he was and so lacked the normal kind of anticipation that you would expect from most kids on their first trip to Walt Disney World. The bus came to a stop at the entryway to the Magic Kingdom and still Ben seemed oblivious as we moved through the bag check security point and then through the turnstiles and underneath the train station. As we walked onto the hub at the base of Main Street, Sara holding his right hand and I holding his left, Ben suddenly went rigid. There directly in front of him, way at the top of Main Street was Cinderella Castle. To the left was Town Hall, to the right was Tony's Restaurant and the Town Square Theater. Over by the Main Street Confectionary, the Dapper Dans, a barbershop quartet, were singing a happy tune to a delighted crowd, while off to the left near the Fire Station a queue of people waited to get hair-cuts at the Harmony Barber Shop. Ben had watched this scene a million times on his video tapes, both in the pre-movie commercials and in some of his sing-a-long tapes, and suddenly it was right in front of him in the real world.

For what seemed like the first time in his life, Benjamin became absolutely *focused* and *present*. He took in all the details of the space – the flagpole in the center of town square, with a line of people there waiting to meet a costumed character; the brightly decorated windows of the Emporium; the train pulling away from the Main Street Station above and behind us. He was soaking it all in with a level of concentration that I had never seen on his face before.

After that slight hesitation he skipped, actually *skipped*, up Main Street towards the hub at the base of Cinderella Castle. Since it was spring break with heavy crowds, the amount of noise and chaos should have been physically overwhelming to him. Instead, he seemed blissfully happy and simply at home.

This was *his* world, and his mother and I were merely visiting there with him.

Our path took us through the Main Street Confectionary, a candy shop filled with every kind of treat imaginable. Overhead a model train chugged along a track suspended from the ceiling, pulling along carts filled with candy. To one side was a display case filled with candied apples and other goodies. Ben's eyes grew as large as saucers, ogling all of the treats around him. The shop connected through to the next space, the Main Street Cinema, where Ben stopped for a while to watch the cartoons being projected on the big screen on the back wall. Onward we went, through shops and alleyways, past Casey's Corner and The Plaza Ice Cream Parlor, and into the hub.

Sometimes the front of Cinderella Castle can be blocked because of musical shows, but at that time no show was happening. We were able to travel up the walkway and through the tunnel at the base of the castle. Ben stopped to admire the murals lining the tunnel walls, a mosaic depiction of moments from the Cinderella story. Emerging from the tunnel, we stepped into the Fantasyland courtyard.

On the left was the Cinderella fountain, to the right Sir Mickey's gift shop, and straight ahead was Cinderella's Golden Carrousel (since renamed Prince Charming's Regal Carrousel). Ben was still blissfully soaking it all in as we decided to take him just around the corner to his very first ride at Walt Disney World: Snow White's Scary Adventures.

Now for a little bit of history about this ride: we didn't know much about it at the time, beyond it seeming like a good, non-threatening attraction to start Ben off with, but I would later discover just how rich in history that particular ride was. *Snow White and the Seven Dwarfs* was the very first feature-length animated film, and at the time it was created, many thought Walt Disney was insane to attempt it. It was even referred to by some as "Disney's Folly". But of course, ultimately Disney was proven right and *Snow White* became a huge hit. In fact, later on during the Second World War when the Walt Disney Company was conscripted by the US Government to make training and propaganda films to support the war effort, it was the theatrical re-release of *Snow White* that kept the company afloat. It was only natural when Walt decided to build a theme park that one of the first attractions should be based on the movie that had garnered so much acclaim.

When Snow White's Adventures was designed at Disneyland in California, it was not intended to be a harmless, fluffy kiddie ride. Rather, it was modeled after the classic Spook Rides of the era, designed to be a scary thrill ride in which the Evil Queen, in her guise as the Old Hag, would jump out and terrorize the riders at every turn. It was dark, noisy, and genuinely scary.

Two decades later, with the opening of Walt Disney World in Florida, Snow White's Adventures was included as an opening day ride at the new Magic Kingdom. It was not identical to its Californian counterpart, largely due to occupying a very different physical space, but thematically it was much the same. Throughout the 70's and 80's, Snow White's Adventures served as a dark and scary thrill ride for the younger set, not as intense as something like Space Mountain but certainly terrifying enough for grade school-aged children. Therein lay the seeds of its own destruction.

The most common complaint about Snow White's Adventures was that it was just too scary for small children whose parents took them on the ride expecting happy singing dwarfs and gentle woodland creatures, but instead got a terrifying descent into madness. This was closely followed by the next most common complaint, "Where the heck was Snow White?" The ride had been designed around the concept that the *rider* was Snow White, living through the experiences of the film and seeing them through her own eyes. As such, Snow White herself only appeared in the name of the ride and on the giant mural in the load/unload area. Baffled theme park visitors did not understand this conceit and were very confused not to see the ride's namesake anywhere within the attraction itself.

Round about 1995, Disney decided that it was time to do a complete reworking of the ride in response to all of the complaints. They changed the name to Snow White's Scary Adventures, inserting a new word in the title as a way to warn unsuspecting parents, while simultaneously making the ride itself substantially *less* scary. The story within the ride was reframed, with Snow White herself appearing no less than four different times throughout the ride. In particular they added a new Happily Ever After ending in which Snow White is seen with Prince Charming riding on a noble white steed towards their shining castle on the horizon. The redesign was considered a great success, and the ride remained in that configuration for the rest of its lifetime, until it was (tragically) closed on May 31st of 2012.

Standing in line on that beautiful morning in March of 2002, we had absolutely no concept of where the next decade would lead us. More immediately, Benjamin himself had no concept of what a theme park attraction was. Growing up in Seattle, there was simply no experience for him to compare it to. He seemed to think the mural was pleasant enough – a lush painting depicting Snow White and all seven dwarfs standing in front of the dwarfs' cottage, with Prince Charming standing off to one side, holding the reins of his proud white stallion as, off in the other direction, the Wicked Queen glares with unbridled jealousy and hatred. Yes, Ben thought the mural was nice enough but he had no idea why we were standing in line. Lines were for things like waiting to pay at the grocery store or waiting to get your fries at McDonald's. The line made no sense to him in this context. Still, he behaved reasonably well for being constrained for 15-20 minutes in the constant switchbacks of the queue, hundreds of other tourists crowded in around him.

Eventually we reached the loading area and were ushered into a mine cart ride vehicle. Ben was still small enough (and heck, *I* was still small enough) that our party of three was able to fit in a single row. With a lurch the mine cart began to roll forward, and Ben was trying to look around in all directions at once in an attempt to figure out what was going on.

As we rolled past the Wishing Well and made the first big turn, Ben's ears suddenly perked up. There was Snow White, sitting in rags on the castle steps, scrubbing the stone with a brush as she sang to the birds around her. The audio was taken directly from that scene in the movie – something I would later learn was a bit of an oddity compared to most of the other rides where audio is re-created and re-imagined from its original source material – and Ben was immediately taken in. As I have said, Ben is extremely audio focused and all of a sudden he was being presented with many of his favorite audio cues from one of his favorite movies.

We turned another corner and passed through a doorway into the dark ride proper, a scene in which the Magic Mirror darkly intoned "Alas, Snow White is the fairest one of all." The Wicked Queen gazed into a mirror and cast a spell, only to spin around suddenly in the guise of the Old Hag, cackling as the occupants of the mine cart passed by.

Onward we rolled, into the Queen's dungeon. Benjamin was positively glowing with excitement. The Old Hag was stirring her bubbling cauldron and dipping the apple into the poison brew. The Huntsman was pleading with Snow White to run and hide. He urged her emphatically, "Go! *Go!!!*"

The music swelled amidst the roll of thunder and a flash of lightning. Snow White was fleeing in terror as the very trees themselves transformed into reaching, grasping fiends. Ben was practically vibrating with intense joy and engagement. Then just as it was possibly all becoming a bit too much, the darkness lifted. We passed through the Friendly Forest and entered the Seven Dwarfs' Cottage.

Sara and I both clapped in time with the dancing dwarfs as they merrily sang their "Silly Song", and Ben began to laugh right along with them. Another turn and Snow White appeared again, accepting the poisoned apple from the Old Hag. "Now *I'm* the fairest in the land!" the evil witch gloated. We once again exited the cottage and passed beneath a pair of vultures while the Old Hag taunted us under the gray skies of a gathering storm. Was Ben worried? Not at all! He was too caught up in all of the sights and sounds flooding around him, for once actually living *inside* one of his movies.

Another turn, and we passed through the Dwarfs' Mine with twinkling gems embedded in the wall as Bashful plaintively cried, "Aww, she's getting away. *Hurry!*" We exited the mine to find the rest of the dwarfs dashing up the rocky bluffs after the Old Hag. She stood on a ledge above us using a stick to lever a huge boulder into our path. At the last moment there was a crash of thunder as a bolt of lightning struck the Old Hag and cast her into the abyss. Suddenly we were through the darkness and back into the peaceful forest. The sunlight dappled down through the branches of the trees as Prince Charming himself leaned down to awaken Snow White with Love's First Kiss.

The music surged as we made the final turn to witness the dwarfs waving goodbye to Snow White and Prince Charming as the young couple rode off to their castle, shining in the distance. Above the final archway Dopey waggled his ears and gave us one last farewell while the mine cart trundled through the doorway and exited back into the load/unload station at the start of the ride. Ben was so happy he hardly knew what to do with himself. His first ride at Walt Disney World — his first ride on Snow White's Scary Adventures — was over. In that moment we knew that we had made the right decision to bring him there.

Chapter 4

Walt Disney World, Continued

Our first day at the Magic Kingdom carried on in much the same way, although none of the other rides were quite so dramatically engaging to Ben. I had brought a digital camera, and as we went to each ride I would take a picture of the façade and then very specifically tell Ben the name of the ride. Throughout the day we visited other attractions like The Many Adventures of Winnie the Pooh, Peter Pan's Flight, and It's a Small World in Fantasyland and Buzz Lightyear's Space Ranger Spin in Tomorrowland. He particularly liked The Haunted Mansion, I think because it had a lot of interesting audio cues throughout the ride. We also toured the great rivers of the world on the Jungle Cruise in Adventureland. Pirates of the Caribbean made him a tiny bit anxious during the one drop, but on the whole he liked it just fine. In particular, he enjoyed a treat he found in the gift shop at the exit from Pirates – a bottle of small, multi-colored candies that came with a treasure map inside. The pirate candy would quickly become a favorite treat of his.

As we left Adventureland and crossed into Frontierland, Ben stopped to watch the logs dropping down the waterfall flowing from the peak of Splash Mountain. He pulled us in the direction of the line, but Sara and I were both a bit nervous. Would he really be able to handle a ride like that, with the huge drop down the waterfall? I had never been on it myself, and the last time Sara had experienced it was years earlier before her family moved away from Florida. She couldn't remember what most of the ride was like, so we asked a few other families as they exited the ride. They all assured us that it was mostly a very tame ride with lots of music and happy animatronics. The only potential concern was the one big drop at the end. Ben was still insistently dragging us towards the line, so we decided to give it a shot.

As it turns out, he really did enjoy the ride. The majority of it was no scarier than the one drop on Pirates, and the ride contained so much music and so many colorful characters for him to soak in. Even as we reached the climax, with its long slow climb in the dark, Ben was just fine. He wasn't particularly thrilled with the big drop itself, but miraculously he shook it off almost right away. He absolutely *loved* the musical riverboat scene after that in the final stretch of the ride.

All in all, we had a very nice day at the Magic Kingdom, and by evening we were on the bus headed back to our resort. The one tricky bit was something that we had noticed that morning. On the route to and from the All Stars resorts, the bus passed a very large McDonald's on Disney property, and we knew from experience that if Ben saw those giant golden arches, he would not let up unless and until we took him there. Given that we did not have a rental car and there were no buses that stopped there, it would have been a very awkward situation. That being the case, Sara and I strategically placed ourselves such that his view out of that side of the bus was completely blocked as we passed by the restaurant.

Once back at the resort, we stopped for some dinner at the dining hall, and then rewarded Ben with a solid hour of swimming in the resort pool. I thought that he would be worn out from the full day walking around the theme park, but his body clock had not adjusted to the time zone change. He still had plenty of energy buzzing around inside him. Eventually he tired of swimming, and we returned to our rooms.

Sara changed Ben into his pajamas, and then he picked up his CD player and headphones and wandered into the bathroom. The room on Sara's side was actually a handicap room, and as such the bathroom was designed to be wheelchair accessible. It was wider than usual — instead of the typical tub/shower combo the bathroom was flat tile with just a shower curtain to separate the walk-in shower space from the rest of the room. Ben really liked the combination of the expanse of the tiled bathroom floor plus the quiet and solitude the room provided. He sat cross-legged listening to his Disney music.

Ben listening to Disney CDs

At some point he was finally ready for sleep. He laid down in one bed while Sara slept in the other. On the other side of the wall I snored my way through the night, exhausted from the very full day.

We were in no particular rush to get up in the morning. Our plan was to spend the day at Epcot. Since we wanted to stay late enough to see the fireworks, we all slept in as late as we could. It was pushing noon before all of us were finally showered or bathed, dressed, and ready to face the world. We had a late breakfast/early lunch at the dining hall and then caught the bus to Epcot. Just like the night before, Sara and I conspired to conceal McDonald's from our little French Fry Monster.

Following a short bus ride, we arrived at Epcot and began touring the Future World section of the park. Epcot is divided into two sections consisting of Future World and the World Showcase. Future World is designed as a variety of pavilions focused on technology and how it is applied to improve our lives. Ben liked Spaceship Earth, which is the giant "golf ball" at the front of the park, and which explores the history of communication from the earliest cave paintings right up through modern day. He had a good time looking at all of the different aquatic life in the Living Seas pavilion, and also particularly liked the life-sized dinosaurs in the Universe of Energy pavilion. Overall, Future World was pretty popular with Ben, and then we moved on to the World Showcase.

The World Showcase consists of eleven different nations celebrating the architecture, food and wares of their respective countries, all circling the World Showcase Lagoon. Purely randomly, we started our way around the lagoon moving in a clockwise direction. Over the course of the next several hours we meandered our way through all of the different countries. In Mexico we went on the El Rio del Tiempo boat ride, which was like a cheesy 1970's video tour brochure of Mexico. (A few years ago that ride was completely changed, transformed into the Gran Fiesta Tour starring The Three Caballeros. It is a nice enough ride, and certainly much higher in quality than the original, but I really miss the campiness of the ride we experienced on that day.) In Norway we went on the Maelstrom and experienced up close the Norwegian love of trolls. We wandered through country after country and had a grand day. In Italy we stopped to watch a Human Statue taunting the passers-by. In France a mime performed for the crowd, and Ben stopped to enjoy the fountains.   By the time we finished our complete circuit of the showcase, it was approaching time for the grand IlluminNations fireworks show, often described by Disney as being the "kiss goodnight". The viewing area where we were at the base of the showcase was fully occupied, so we continued on in the same direction, passing Mexico for the second time that day. Somewhere along the shore between Norway and China we finally found a spot to stop and watch the show, which was absolutely amazing. The show featured stunning fireworks, dramatic music, the heat and intensity of the Inferno Barge, dancing water fountains at water level, laser beams slicing through the clouds of smoke at treetop level, and all of the lights framing the buildings of the different countries around the world. It was hypnotic, and Ben loved every bit of it.

Once the show ended, we took a bathroom break to let the crowds disperse a bit. Once the crowds were sufficiently thinned we started to walk back towards the park entrance by the way that we had come, which was moving counter-clockwise around the lagoon. Ben grew extremely agitated. He grabbed both Sara and I by the hands, to pull us in the other direction. When we tried to move him towards the park exit, his agitation began to build towards a full-on meltdown. Clearly something very important to him was in the other direction, so we relented and let him lead the way.

He proceeded to walk us entirely around the World Showcase for the second time that day. Despite the fact that the pathway to Spaceship Earth and the park exit had only been perhaps 100 yards away, Ben insisted that we walk the complete 1.3 miles around the entire promenade in order to reach the exact same pathway. For whatever reason, Ben had decided that no matter the circumstance the *only* proper direction to move around the Showcase was clockwise. Ultimately we did finally make it out of the park and were able to rest our feet on the bus ride back to the hotel. There was another late night dip in the resort pool, and then we all fell into bed.

We had intended to spend the next morning at the Animal Kingdom, but we got such a late start that we wound up going to Disney MGM Studios instead. Ben had fun, he was still as active and engaged as he had been all week, but there were no particular moments that stood out.

For our final day of vacation we returned to the Magic Kingdom. Not surprisingly the first place he wanted to go was Snow White's Scary Adventures for several more rides. A few hours later, after rides on a few other attractions, we found ourselves stopping for lunch at the Columbia Harbor House restaurant located on the border between Fantasyland and Liberty Square. After getting our food, we found a table upstairs in the section that looked down towards the Haunted Mansion, Tom Sawyer Island, and part of Big Thunder Mountain Railroad. Off in the distance we could even see a bit of Splash Mountain.

As we sat eating, I got out the digital camera to show Ben pictures of the different ride entrances so he could show us what he wanted to do next. Up until this point in the trip, as excited and as engaged as he was, he had still remained largely non-verbal. Looking at those pictures, however, he started actually naming the rides. "Haunted Mansion! Splash! Snow White!!"

His mother and I were stunned. We had been thrilled with how much he was enjoying the trip, but having him spontaneously speak was completely unprecedented. We were both nearly in tears as Ben grinned and pointed at pictures on the camera screen, shouting out the name of each ride. That was the moment when I knew right down to my core that Walt Disney World was the single biggest piece of magic that had ever entered Ben's life.

We spent the remainder of the day visiting whichever rides Ben asked for, and then finished off with the fireworks show. Once the music faded and the last of the smoke cleared, we made our way to the hotel room to begin packing. We had one last night at Disney, and then the next morning we were on a flight home to Seattle and back to our regular lives. We knew we would be returning to Walt Disney World. The only question was when?

Chapter 5

Back in the Real World

With the big vacation over, I returned to my empty apartment in Seattle and pondered life. I went to work and wrote code. I went home and either watched TV alone or maybe hung out with some friends. Weekends I spent with Ben. I treasured every moment with him.

One evening I stopped by Sara's place to drop off a jacket for Ben that had inadvertently been left at my apartment the previous weekend. Ben was so excited to see me he ran in circles and spun in place before finally giving me a big hug and then turned his cheek towards me so that I could give him a smooch. Then he disappeared into his bedroom while I had a brief conversation with Sara. When he reappeared, it was to barrel into the living room, dragging his packed suitcase behind him. He was all set and ready to come home with me. It made me both happy and sad at the same moment – happy because it was gratifying to see him express how much he loved me; sad because I knew I had to deny him. I hated to have to leave him behind that night, but he had school the next morning and in any case he was on mom time.

Another time, a few weeks later, I was out and about with Ben on the weekend doing some shopping. We went into a bookstore and he started to get a little out of hand. I would usually let him run around a bit in a store as long as he wasn't plowing into people or otherwise causing a problem, but I did have to occasionally rein him in when he got too worked up. So I got down on his level, looked him straight in the eye, and said, "Shhhhh....".

He immediately got a gleam in his eye, a huge grin on his face, and then he turned his head and pressed his ear directly onto my mouth. I kept going "shhhhh" into his ear, and he put his arms around me and just enjoyed the white noise. When I stopped, he immediately grabbed my chin and faced me towards him, saying, "Daddy. I want. Shhh. Please!" I did it some more, and after a few minutes of breathing heavily into my child's ear, he was ready to move on.

A while later we were in a different store when he asked for "shhh" again, only this time he wanted to look into my mouth while I was doing it. He stuck his finger in my mouth, running it along my teeth to feel the sound. Fair enough, he had clean hands. No big deal.

Then he wanted to taste the sound.

Most of the time I am fairly willing to indulge him as he explores new things, but I draw the line at my son trying to French kiss me....

Spring turned to summer, and the difference between Ben-At-Disney and Ben-In-The-Real-World was very stark indeed. Some days he would become extremely difficult, running off in stores or throwing fits. Every now and then it would stretch me to the very end of my patience. He had one vocalization in particular that he would use: a whiny ululating sound that he would make when he wasn't getting what he wanted, which seemed specifically chosen to grate on my nerves. On more than one occasion I would need to lock him in a room – not as punishment, but so that he would be in a space where I knew he was completely safe while I closed myself in the bathroom and screamed into a pillow to vent my frustration. I would think about his maddening behaviors, and then think about the Ben that I had seen skipping his way through the Magic Kingdom, and I began to wonder if maybe he actually belonged there.

I tentatively brought it up with Sara, and she confessed that she had been having the same thoughts. It seemed insane, but we were actually discussing uprooting both of our households and moving permanently to the opposite corner of the country. And for what? So that our profoundly disabled child could go play in theme parks year round? It seemed ludicrous, yet neither of us could get it out of our heads.

Ultimately we decided to accept the idea that moving was a possibility, but that the only rational thing to do would be to plan a second vacation to Walt Disney World and see if he showed the same response again. If he didn't, then no harm, no foul. We would have an answer and abandon the idea of the move. If he did, then we would start making concrete plans. Given that we both needed some time to save up enough money for another trip, we decided to schedule it for February of 2003. In the meantime we would just carry on as normal.

Time marched on, as it is wont to do. Summer turned to fall. Ben's behavior and sleep habits were all over the map. We struggled to work with doctors to find the correct balance of medications to help him be happier and less anxious without turning him into a drugged-out zombie. His lack of sleep and manic behavior was not only bad for him, but it was detrimental to my own mental health and I am sure to his mother's as well. One night it got so bad, I wrote the following in my personal journal. This text is absolutely unchanged from what I wrote that night aside from being edited for profanity:

> *It's four o'clock in the <profanity> morning. I have not slept. I do not have insomnia, I have an autistic son that I am inches away from throwing out the <profanity> window. My house is a shambles. I have systematically gone through and removed every light bulb from every light fixture to keep him from turning on the lights. I have shut down the power strip in the living room to keep him from turning on the tv. I have been trying to get him to go to bed for*

*the past seven hours. I have bodily carried him into
the bedroom and placed him in his bed more times
than I can remember. My jaw aches from my
grinding teeth. My stomach is in an ulcerous knot. I
want to scream at the top of my lungs. I want to
throw him across the room. I want to <profanity>
go to sleep.*

This was followed a few hours later with:

*Ben finally fell asleep at 5:30. He was up again by
9:00. He woke me up by figuring out how to plug
the television back in, turning it on to static, and
then turning the volume up as high as it would go.*

I am not proud of how crazed his behavior made me. I *am* grateful that I was able to hold it together enough to not take out my frustrations on him. I really and truly can see how a person can tip over into a very dark place and do simply unthinkable things to an innocent child. It is no defense, but I do have a measure of compassion for others who have found themselves driven to that edge and beyond.

But I also know that Benjamin was every bit as frustrated and miserable as I was, and for him it was even worse because he had no way to understand it. His brain simply did not create the neural connections necessary to fully comprehend the world around him. Although he was physically nine years old and rapidly approaching ten, mentally he was much closer to being a toddler. He needed all the help he could get, and it was my job as his father to move Heaven and Earth to get him that help.

By the end of September we finally seemed to have found a mix of medications that allowed him to sleep reasonably well and which helped to minimize his meltdowns. This of course made everybody involved very happy indeed.

One Friday night I saw a chance to perhaps rekindle a bit of the Disney experience when I saw that our local swimming pool was advertising a "Dive In Movie". They strung a movie screen across one side of the pool and then projected *The Lion King* onto it during an open swim. Disney and swimming at the same time? How could this *not* be a hit?

Ben and I got there a bit early, which turned out to be a good thing. He was apprehensive about going into the building at first and spent about a half hour watching through the exterior bay window that looked into the pool as people were swimming laps. By the time the cashier at the front desk was ready to start letting people in for the open swim, Ben had settled down completely and was ready to go inside.

When the movie started, his jaw literally dropped. It was Simba! On a *really big screen*! In a *SWIMMING POOL!!!* Yeah, he was very happy with this idea. He got into the pool, and before long he discovered that it was possible to swim over *behind* the screen and see the movie backwards. He thought that was pretty dang cool.

He spent the last half hour of the movie out in the deep end of the pool where it was much less crowded. He was swimming around in 12 feet of water without a problem and having a great time. When the movie ended he got out of the water with no argument. We dried off and dressed and then headed home. As an added bonus, he was so worn out from swimming that he went to bed early and slept like a rock. The power of Disney had struck again. I remained convinced that a move to Orlando was the right thing to do.

A few weeks later I finally tentatively raised the issue with my direct supervisor at work. The biggest hurdle for me in moving was that I would very likely have a hard time finding a software development job in Central Florida, and even if I did find a job it would almost certainly be at a substantial pay cut from my current salary. On the other hand, absolutely nothing I did at work actually required me to physically be in the office. If ever a job was ripe for telecommuting, it was writing code.

One day an opportunity finally presented itself for me to have a conversation about it with my boss. I explained exactly why I felt it was so important for me to move my son to Florida, and I described exactly how I felt I could manage my time and communication to be able to continue to do my current job. I was, of course, nervous about what his response would be. Thankfully, he was very receptive to the idea. From his perspective, although it was certainly not impossible to bring in a new person and get him or her up to speed, it would definitely be less expensive to keep me doing what I was doing. More importantly, he felt that I had already proven my ability to work remotely and remain productive since I had done exactly that on several occasions while working from home for any number of reasons. Now that I had the support of my direct manager, the next move was to wait until after we came back from our second Disney trip in February and then begin lobbying up the management food chain to get approval.

Naturally, the universe does not like it when life gets too easy or too predictable. I was on a direct course to moving 3,000 miles across the country to go live in a theme park, and my job and career were still on track. Everything was moving smoothly. So, of course, that's exactly when I picked to fall in love.

Honestly, it wasn't my plan. For several years after my divorce I didn't even date. In the previous year or two I had finally started going out on the occasional date here and there. There were even two women (on separate occasions) whom I had gone out with fairly steadily for a couple months. But in the end those relationships, for whatever reason, never caught fire. With only eight months to go until I uprooted my entire life, I was surely not about to fall in love now. Silly me.

I had originally met Kristine almost four years earlier through a group of fans for Pat Cashman, a local Seattle radio and television personality. As Kris tells it, it was love at first sight for her. Because I am considerably more a complete idiot, it took me several years to catch up with that idea. We got to know each other slowly between 1998 and 2002, spending that time first as acquaintances and then later friends. She was always fantastic around Ben and seemed to instinctively know how to handle him. On several occasions Kris and I had gone out to see movies, plays, even the ballet. In fact, earlier in the year, we had even had a brief fling that I managed to completely screw up through my total failure at communication.

As Christmas of 2002 came around, I asked her to come with me to my company holiday party. We had a lovely evening. And then a lovely day after that. And then another, and another. Simply put, she was (and is) an amazingly comfortable person. She just... fits. By the middle of January, I finally came to realize that I was actually in love. This was the person with whom I wanted to spend the rest of my life. Which, of course, presented a serious problem.

Several people told me to just relax and enjoy the present, not to worry about the future. Kris was one of those people. All our cards were on the table, nobody was being deceived, and so I tried to go with it and enjoy the moment.

One evening I had a conversation about it with Trisha, a mutual friend of ours. I told her that I was considering breaking it off with Kris because I didn't think I had any right to ask her to uproot her entire life and move across the country with me. Trisha just gave me a piercing stare and then said, "Don't you think that's *her* decision to make?" As usual, Trisha was absolutely correct.

From my personal journal dated January 12, 2003:

> *The fact is I just feel *right* when I am with her. It's not a fireworks and romantic violins kind of thing, just a general sense of wellbeing. Watching a movie with her snuggled up next to me; driving down a country road with her hand lightly brushing my kneecap or my shoulder; sitting around chit-chatting with other friends with a comfortable ease together; — it just all feels right and good.*

Chapter 6

Walt Disney World, Take Two

In the blink of an eye it was February of 2003 and time for our second visit to Walt Disney World. I left Kris behind in Seattle with the promise that I would call as often as possible, and then headed to the airport with my son and my ex-wife. That's not weird, right?

The flight from Seattle to Orlando was blissfully uneventful. Ben did very well going through airport security, listening and following directions at least as much as he could understand. All of us had to be wanded separately by the security agents, and Ben did very well staying seated in a chair while they scanned Sara. On the whole, the security people were very nice and understanding of Ben's autism.

On the flight, Ben passed the time reading, watching movies, and listening to CDs. We let him get up to stretch his legs a few times, and he was very good about not bothering other passengers. Certainly, he got a little fidgety by the last hour of the flight, but not enough to cause any problems. Truth be told, he was better than several of the other children on the plane. A flight to Orlando is virtually guaranteed to be loaded up with kids all keyed up for a trip to Disney, and I thought that Ben acquitted himself well in that environment. Finally we arrived in Florida, gathered up our bags, and took the shuttle once again to stay at the All Star Music resort. By the time we checked into our rooms and settled in, we were all exhausted and ready for a good night's sleep.

Ben slept like a rock that night and didn't want to get up the following morning. We finally dragged him out of bed at 11am, threw him in the tub, and then got him dressed and headed out for the day. After a quick swing through the dining hall to get some breakfast, we caught the bus out to the Magic Kingdom. From where our hotel was located, the Magic Kingdom is the farthest out of all the parks, but even so the bus ride was only about ten minutes. As we arrived at the main gate, the overcast sky had started to turn to rain. People were walking around in ponchos, or with big umbrellas, and the park was *much* less crowded than the last time we had been there. Going on a rainy day, and not during spring break, was definitely working in our favor.

Ben was thrilled to be there, practically dragging us through the gates and on to Main Street. Rather than walk the street, we wound up taking a horse-driven carriage up Main Street, right to the hub at the foot of Cinderella Castle. Ben was a man on a mission. He knew where he was, and he knew where he wanted to be — Snow White's Scary Adventures. It was the first ride he had ever been on at Walt Disney World, and he made a beeline for it again that day. He was just so overjoyed to see his ride again. It was as if the last year just melted away. I suspect that if we had left it up to him, we would have just spent the rest of our vacation right there, going non-stop, around and around, on Snow White's Scary Adventures.

But of course, we insisted that he had to see and do other things, if not for his own sanity, then at least for ours. In rapid succession we went on Snow White, Winnie the Pooh, Peter Pan, and It's a Small World. We also made a side trip over to Tomorrowland for a ride on the Tomorrowland Transit Authority, formerly called the People Mover. We would have gone on Buzz Lightyear but it was closed for refurbishment.

Of course even on rainy off-season days at the Magic Kingdom, "in rapid succession" means more like three hours. We were all ready for lunch and a chance to sit down for a bit so we went to Ben's favorite restaurant in the park, the Columbia Harbour House. From Ben's point of view the restaurant had two huge selling points: 1) they have fries, and 2) they have a table on the second floor – the same table where he had amazed us the previous year by naming rides while looking at pictures on the camera – which has a view onto the courtyard for the Haunted Mansion and across the way to Big Thunder Mountain Railroad. He had no desire to actually go on Thunder Mountain, but watching from that window he liked the scale of it. He munched his fries, drank his juice, and watched the coaster whoosh by.

After lunch we naturally went right to the Haunted Mansion. I remember that the cast member working the ride entrance that day was particularly good with his ghoulish gallows humor. After Haunted Mansion we cut across Liberty Square and over to Adventureland for Pirates of the Caribbean and the Jungle Cruise. Not surprisingly, the gift shop at the exit from Pirates had the single prize Ben had been angling for all day: the pirate bottle filled with candy and a treasure map.

He was delighted when we purchased it for him. As soon as we were out of the shop, Ben very carefully took the plastic wrap off of the lid and handed it to Sara to throw away. He is always very meticulous about not littering. Then he unscrewed the cap, took out the map, and also handed that to Sara to throw away. That done, he put the cap back on the bottle and held his treasure. He would save opening the bottle again until he got back to the hotel room for the night and could dump it out on the bed in a big pile of primary colors and begin sorting them.

It was after Pirates that the day took a downturn. He pulled us over to Splash Mountain again, watching the big drop into the Briar Patch and eager to go on the ride. Since he had been on it last year we didn't even hesitate. Unfortunately, the big drop really scared him this time. I think it was because last year he didn't actually get splashed, but this time he got a face full of cold water. He was sobbing in fear, and unfortunately the ride goes on for a bit after the drop. He sat in the ride vehicle crying and begging to be "all done", but it took several minutes to complete the ride and get out.

From that point on and for the rest of the day, he was always either in tears or else close to it. He wanted nothing to do with Mickey's ToonTown Fair and passed on the chance to meet Cinderella. At one point he even turned down French fries. He was seriously Not Happy. We cut back over to Fantasyland in an attempt to get him back into his comfort zone. By now it was less than an hour to park closing and all of his favorite rides would likely be walk-ons. The majority of park visitors would already be making their way towards Main Street and the exit. He did another round of Snow White, Pooh, Peter Pan, It's a Small World, Snow White again, working his way back to being happy. Unfortunately the fireworks at closing time spooked him again, and he just wanted out of the park. He wasn't upset anymore, he was just tired, his feet hurt (if he was anything like me), and he wanted to get back to the hotel and get some rest. I couldn't really blame him.

When we returned to the hotel room, Ben was happy to get into his pajamas and then sit on his bed listening to music and piling up the candy from his pirate bottle. Sara went to the dining hall to pick us up some dinner, and by 9:30 we were all ready for bed. During last year's visit, Ben never adjusted to the time change and consistently was up until 2am, but that night he was yawning and ready to lie down and get some sleep. Overall it was a good day, even with the Splash Mountain fiasco.

Unfortunately the dark shadows from the second half of the day continued to loom over us that night. None of us slept well at all. I woke up at 3:30am and was never able to get back to sleep. Meanwhile on the other side of the wall in their room, Ben was up and down all night and never got any real sleep either. Of course, if he wasn't sleeping then neither was Sara. It was afternoon before we were all up and ready to venture out, which as it happens, was right when an unexpected torrential downpour began. It was another two hours before the rainstorm eventually cleared. By mid-afternoon we finally gathered up our supplies and made our way to Epcot.

In retrospect, we probably should have just bagged the entire day and gone back to bed.

As soon as we got on the bus to Epcot, Ben started sobbing. He was miserable and couldn't explain why. We had hoped that maybe getting him some fries would calm him down, but that didn't work. We tried taking him on Spaceship Earth, which he had loved the previous year, but he spent the whole ride crying with his face buried in his mother's lap. The poor kid was stuck in a feedback loop. I know that he hates being that way, but he can't stop himself. Eventually he began to calm down a little, which then led to him finally being willing to eat something. After a plate of fries and a cup of juice, he started to perk up a little.

Following lunch we went back and rode Spaceship Earth again. This time Ben was watching everything intently. He wasn't exactly happy, but at least he wasn't miserable. This was a great improvement.

From there we went to see the aquariums in The Living Seas, which he seemed to enjoy. He actually led us there, retracing the same route we took last year. He even had a little bit of a bounce in his step. Our next stop was The Land, which we had not gone to the previous year. One of the attractions in that part of the park is called Living With the Land, which is a very calm ride through a bunch of stuff about food production and innovative holistic growing techniques. As soon as we got on the boat Ben began sobbing again. He was clearly terrified to be on a boat ride again, the shadow of Splash Mountain the day before looming large. Thankfully the ride ended, and Ben calmed down a little once we were actually off the boat.

By this point Sara and I were both beginning to reconsider the notion of moving to Orlando. The whole point was to make him happy, and to use his love of the parks as a lever to help him become more socialized. The whole dream was beginning to evaporate right before our eyes. Usually Central Florida has very clear blue skies. On that day the uncharacteristically overcast skies were either mimicking or mocking our own pervasive feelings of doom and gloom. Still, we soldiered on hoping to salvage something out of the day.

The next closest attraction was Journey Into Imagination. That ride had been closed the previous year, so once again Ben was anxious because he didn't know what to expect. It wasn't a boat ride, though, so he relaxed a little and seemed to enjoy it at least a little bit. It appeared we were moving in the right direction. We decided to move on to the World Showcase, being sure to approach it in a clockwise direction in order to prevent a repeat of the previous year's frustrations.

As with last year, we went into the giant Pyramid in Mexico and took him on El Rio del Tiempo. Although it is a boat ride, is very placid with no drops or splashing. Even still, he was absolutely miserable. Right next door to Mexico in the World Showcase is Norway, with another water ride called The Maelstrom. We elected to skip that, even though he had liked it the previous year. The ride has a part where the boat is stopped by a troll and then pushed backwards down a waterfall. Although it is a comparatively small drop, we just didn't see the point of trying it when he was clearly terrified of water rides.

Here's the funny thing about autistic kids: a decision is made to prevent a problem, and it winds up coming back with sharp teeth looking for a butt to bite.

As we walked through the World Showcase he just wasn't happy. He alternated between being either in a zombie-like state or else descending into sobbing hysteria. Honestly, this was exactly what I had feared would happen the previous year. None of the places that he had loved the year before did anything for him this year. He was plainly distressed about something but didn't have any words to express it. We stopped for dinner in Japan, and he cried all the way through the meal and finally begged, "I want *bus!*"

We resigned ourselves to returning to the hotel early, giving him some medication to calm him down, and getting him to bed. We hoped that the entire day was a result of lack of sleep.

He led us around the end of the World Showcase, but then instead of heading towards Spaceship Earth and the park entrance, he pulled us back towards Mexico. When we tried to correct him and point him towards the way to the buses, he was absolutely insistent that we go˙ the other way back to the beginning of the World Showcase. He seemed to know exactly what he wanted, so we let him lead the way.

He passed by Mexico and wanted nothing to do with going inside the Pyramid again. When we arrived in Norway, he insisted on pulling us to the entrance for the Maelstrom. When we balked, he pulled harder. Needless to say, we were very confused. After spending all day panicking at even the mildest of boat rides, it made no rational sense that he wanted to go on a boat ride with a substantial drop in it. But there it was in front of us, and he could not have been clearer about what he wanted.

As near as we could figure, he merely needed to retrace everything we had done the previous year. Failing to match that pattern was causing him significant distress, even more distress than his current fear of boat rides. He rode the Maelstrom, and although he wasn't exactly enjoying himself, he did seem to have an air of grim determination.

With the ride over, we moved on. We tried to turn him around and head him back towards the park exit, but once again he was adamant on heading further into the World Showcase. This, at least, did not surprise us; he had already made it abundantly clear that the World Showcase was only to be navigated in a clockwise manner. As we walked around the world for the second time, he would pause occasionally to look out at the lake and just stand and contemplate the view. He still didn't seem particularly happy, but at least he wasn't crying anymore.

We finished our second lap, and this time he was ready to head towards the exit. That was when I made my big mistake. I stopped to take a picture of Spaceship Earth, and had to fiddle with the settings on my camera because the first picture turned out awful. I thought Ben and Sara were right behind me, but when I turned around they were gone. I thought to myself that I must have spent more time taking the picture than I realized. Ben had probably pulled Sara forward to Spaceship Earth for another ride. I headed that way, still scanning the thinning crowd ahead and behind me, looking for any sign of them. I arrived at the entrance, and asked the woman working there if she might have noticed a blond-haired woman enter with a child in just the last minute or two? "Was it a little blonde haired boy? They just got on."

Although we had brought 2-way radios for the trip, we did not have them with us just then for reasons that I no longer remember. Although I owned a cell phone Sara did not yet have one, so calling her was not an option. We also had not had the presence of mind to agree on a place to meet if we became separated. The best thing I could figure to do was to stand next to the exit ramp from the ride and wait.

Sure enough, fifteen minutes later a blonde woman exited the ride with a little blonde haired boy. Unfortunately, it wasn't Sara and Ben.

As my British friends would say, "Oh bloody hell."

I walked outside, figuring that at this point my best option was to take a bus back to the hotel and hope that Sara and Ben did the same thing. Through sheer dumb luck, they were walking by just as I walked out the door. I explained what had happened to me, and it turned out that as I was taking the picture Ben had pulled her into a gift shop. By the time they came out I was gone. They had spent the past 20 minutes searching for me and were just about to give up when I stumbled into them.

We finally made it back to the hotel. After much winding down, Ben finally went to sleep. Thankfully, he slept like a rock.

The next morning, after a solid night's sleep, Ben seemed to be in a great mood. This, combined with the fact that the Disney MGM Studios had no boat rides, boded well for the day.

Then we got on the bus.

Right away the sobbing started again, like an unhappy replay of the previous day. We began making contingency plans to return to the hotel and spend a quiet day in the room, with maybe a few visits to the swimming pool. We didn't want to give up quite yet, though, so we carried on. When we got to the park, the first thing we did was go on the Great Movie Ride inside the replica of Grauman's Chinese Theatre. He had a few shaky moments during the early part of the ride with the gangsters and the cowboys, but overall he seemed to enjoy himself. About halfway through the ride we came around a turn to discover Sorcerer Mickey and the Enchanted Brooms dancing to music from The Sorcerer's Apprentice. Seeing his old buddy Sorcerer Mickey seemed to cheer Ben up, and by the time we were finished there it was already time for lunch.

We had a reservation at the Sci-Fi Dine-In Theater, so that was our next destination. Let me just say this: Coolest. Restaurant. Ever. This place absolutely rocks. The tables are actually converted cars that are parked at a circa-1950's drive-in theater. The screen runs a never-ending reel of trailers for bad science fiction flicks like Plan 9 From Outer Space, Catwomen from Mars, The Amazing Colossal Man, and Invasion of the Saucer Men. The trailers are interspersed with period animated shorts that have a science fiction theme as well as authentic reels from drive-ins advertising the snack bar and issuing messages from the management. On top of all that, the food is genuinely good. Ben definitely liked the restaurant, munching on fries and watching the movie screen. It makes me wish there were still drive-ins operating where I could take him.

After lunch we continued to tour the park, seeing the live performance of Beauty and the Beast and walking through the One Man's Dream exhibit of Walt Disney memorabilia. Ben was in a fine mood, and he pulled us directly down to the Backlot Tour which precipitated the worst part of the day. Part of the tour involves going through Catastrophe Canyon where, among other things, a giant flood of water crashes down towards the tram. Ben completely panicked at the millions of gallons of water flooding all around us, and it took over an hour to calm him down.

We spent the rest of the afternoon roaming around the park, spending some time at the Animation Studio Tour before wrapping up the day by taking him to see the nightly Fantasmic show. Unfortunately the show takes place in a lake and contains a great deal of water effects. Ben was at first afraid and upset, but slowly began to realize that he wasn't going to get splashed. The show is essentially Mickey's dream and an attempt by the villains to corrupt his dream and take control. Mostly it is an excuse to show off the entire library of Disney heroes and villains, including a very large fire-breathing dragon. Ben watched the whole thing, often with his head cocked kind of sideways as if he just wasn't sure about what he was seeing. Although he was on the edge of panicking much of the time, he was never so afraid that he stopped watching or tried to get away. It was kind of the same way one might approach a fearsome-looking dog when the owner gives his assurances that his dog won't bite.

Once the show was over, we took a bus back to the hotel. Upon returning to the room, Ben was happy and bouncy. As a matter of fact, he even went up to Sara at one point and very clearly asked for peanut butter. It had been months since the last time he had been willing to eat peanut butter, and here he was asking for it out of the blue. We were both floored, and Sara rapidly whipped out the peanut butter and rice cakes to make him a meal. He wolfed that down along with some cookies and graham crackers, and drained a cup of juice. He was in an absolutely delightful mood, and shortly thereafter he dropped off to sleep.

Chapter 7

Walt Disney World, Take Two – Continued

Originally our plan for the next day, Wednesday, had been to go to the Animal Kingdom during the day, and then Downtown Disney in the evening. Sara had been pondering Ben's responses to the bus rides in the morning, and she wondered if maybe the reason he was getting upset on the bus was that he wanted to go back to the Magic Kingdom and was frustrated when he realized the bus wasn't going there. We decided to change our plans. Rather than go to Animal Kingdom on Wednesday and a second day at Epcot on Thursday, we would go again to the Magic Kingdom on Wednesday and to the Animal Kingdom on Thursday. On Friday we would spend a third day at the Magic Kingdom.

It seemed like a reasonable hypothesis. In the morning we loaded up and headed off for the Magic Kingdom with Ben smiling and happy all the way. He was happy on the bus for the entire trip and was grinning and pulling us onward when we arrived at the main gate. It seemed apparent that his mother's guess was right on the nose.

When we came on the first day of our trip it was overcast and rainy, so we had pretty much skipped Main Street and went directly to Cinderella's Castle. This time the sun was shining brightly and we took the time to wander up the avenue. Ben was very clear on which direction he wanted to go, heading straight for Fantasyland and Snow White's Scary Adventures. We swung by Pooh first to get Fastpasses (tickets that give you a specific time to return so that you don't have to stand in line as long), and then Ben took us straight to his favorite ride. He was bouncing and happy and obviously exactly where he wanted to be. He enjoyed the ride immensely, and then we carried on with some other attractions around the park – It's A Small World, Haunted Mansion, Pooh, etc. — before sitting down for some lunch. Ben was in a great mood, very calm and focused. He had gotten a little upset on Haunted Mansion, but only because the cars stopped twice, which happens occasionally due to loading or unloading issues. Once the cars were moving again he was fine.

After lunch we went to Adventureland to ride Pirates of the Caribbean. This was the one and only disaster of the day. He had definitely become terrified of water rides, even ones he has ridden before and loved. He was miserable during the entire ride. Walking away from that, he didn't want anything to do with the Jungle Cruise which he had always loved before. It seemed like Splash Mountain had really shaken him, and I hated to see him not want to go on other peaceful water rides because of it.

To calm him down a bit, we went back to Fantasyland where he rode Peter Pan's Flight.

Thankfully he returned to his normal bouncy self. We had taken an afternoon break in the Columbia Harbour House where Ben was snacking on some fries and looking at pictures of the different ride entrances. When I showed him the picture for Snow White's Scary Adventures, he immediately lit up with a huge smile and grabbed the camera from me to get a closer look. He was just so happy it was downright infectious. Not long after that we left the restaurant intending to go to the bus terminals in order to head back to the hotel. Ben had other plans. He grabbed my hand, which was a first for the day since he had been mostly clinging to Sara all week, held out my camera almost like a divining rod, and made a beeline for Snow White.

This last time through I actually videotaped the whole ride. I didn't tape Ben; I just pointed the camera forward and captured the entire ride from standing in line all the way through to exiting the ride cart. This was in the days before YouTube, when there was not instantly-accessible video available for anything and everything at a moment's demand – I know, hard to imagine those dark days! – and I wanted to be able to bring something home from the trip for Ben to enjoy.

By this point it had become readily apparent that while the Magic Kingdom in general was a motivator for Ben, it was the charms of Disney's original princess that truly enchanted Ben and captured his heart. I really hoped that having this particular recording at home would help keep him interested and engaged during the half year between when we returned home to Seattle and when we intended to permanently move to Orlando.

With that final ride on Snow White's Scary Adventures complete, we exited the park and took the bus back to the hotel. Ben was happy and talkative the whole way, which was such a delightful change over the previous two days. For this visit we actually had a rental car so our plan was to go back to the room, drop off a few things, and then take Ben somewhere for dinner off property, followed by a visit to Downtown Disney on the way back. Dinner was very nice, and Ben surrounded himself with comfort items. To his right was his CD player, with headphones on, listening to Disney tunes. In the center was a plate of fries which he devoured. To his left was my camera with video screen turned on and showing the picture of the Snow White ride entrance. Never has there been a happier kid. After dinner we spent about an hour at Downtown Disney, the big shopping complex on the eastern edge of Disney property, and Ben seemed to be enjoying himself there as well. The spell cast by Snow White seemed to be very long-lasting, and had quite literally transformed Ben into a blissfully happy and contented boy.

Eventually we returned to our hotel and Ben began to wind down. He got into his pajamas and then lay on my bed listening to music and looking at the Snow White picture. After a while Sara got ready for bed and went over to her room to lie down and go to sleep. Ben actually stayed in my bed with me, the first time he had done so on the entire trip, and he drifted off to sleep listening to music. His deep, contented sleep was infectious. Not long after that I drifted off as well. That night *everybody* got a good night's sleep for the first time in days.

The next morning Ben bounced out of bed, took his morning bath, and was ready to go out on a new adventure – his very first visit to the Animal Kingdom (and ours as well). It really is a fabulous park. It doesn't feel like a theme park at all, but it doesn't quite feel like a zoo either. The park is filled with interesting little nooks and paths to wander down, and everywhere there are different animals and plants to see. Ben was interested and engaged the entire time as we meandered our way towards the African-themed section and then went on the safari tour. He had a good time riding along on the safari looking out at the scenery and definitely watching the different animals on the plains. After the safari we also took a stroll through the wildlife preserve and saw things ranging from apes to meerkats. The entire feel was very calm and inviting. Ben was clearly enjoying himself. He particularly liked both the elephants and the giraffes, probably because they were just so darn big!

Following a quick lunch we moved on to Asia where we saw several tigers ("Shere Khan!" exclaimed Ben), and a variety of other animals. We wisely chose to skip the Kali River Rapids – God only knows how Ben would react to a white-water thrill ride given his Splash Mountain-induced phobia.

We were running short on time. The Animal Kingdom was closing at 5pm, so we spent the last hour or so in Dinoland U.S.A., which Ben absolutely loved. Sara took him on the Triceratops Spin, which is very similar to the Dumbo ride at Fantasyland only with big, friendly green triceratops to ride in. I was a little unsure how Ben would respond, but he adored it. I even managed to get at least one decent picture of them going by. Time was running out. Both Sara and I wanted to go on Dinosaur. We knew that Ben would be traumatized if we tried to take him on that particular attraction. Fortunately they let us do a kid swap, so I rode it first and then as soon as I got off Sara walked on while I sat with Ben. It is a great ride, but very dark and loud with big scary dinosaurs leaping out at you to eat you. Ben would have been traumatized by it, but we both thoroughly enjoyed it.

With that we wrapped up our successful day at the Animal Kingdom and elected to not push our luck and instead simply return to the hotel to have a quiet, relaxing evening. Some dinner, maybe a dip in the pool, let Ben unwind and maybe even get to bed early that night.

It was February 13th, and by then I was particularly missing Kris. I was glad that Ben was having such a great time. I certainly enjoyed sharing that experience with him, but it was becoming very trying spending so much time with my ex-wife when I would much rather have been with the woman whom I loved. As soon as Ben was successfully bathed and put to bed, I left him in the care of his mother while I went out to get a little quiet time for myself.

The day before setting out on this vacation, Kris had come over to my place to spend the evening with me. It was a very lovely and comfortable night, and then as she was leaving she handed me a card and instructed me not to open it until Valentine's Day. At that moment I was speechless. I knew that I looked like a total loser, having completely forgotten to have a card for her as well, but the truth was that two weeks earlier I had gone to the florist up the street from the office where she worked and arranged to have a bouquet delivered. I had gone locally for the particular reason that I could fill out a card in my own handwriting so she would know how much I loved her and that the flowers weren't just a last minute thing. As Kris was handing me the card, *I* knew that I had Valentine's Day covered, but at that particular moment I didn't look so hot. Such is the pain of a devious mind.

Now here it was, just after midnight as I sat in a deck chair by the empty resort pool, and I finally opened the card Kris had given to me. It really made my day, and made me that much more eager to return home and be with her.

The next morning we got up and headed off to The Magic Kingdom for a third day. Ben was overjoyed — it was beautiful, warm and sunny, and he went skipping onto Main Street and then right to Fantasyland. Snow White. FastPass for Pooh. Peter Pan was closed due to mechanical problems. Haunted Mansion. The morning flew by. Soon it was time for lunch in the restaurant on the second floor inside Cinderella Castle. It was during lunch we discovered that Ben was starting to get frustrated because his headphones were shorting out. He wore the headphones as a way to calm himself by quieting down the noisy world around him, and now they were not working. With it being his very last day at the Magic Kingdom, I did not want this problem to snowball into a huge issue. I left Ben in Sara's care, and went off in search of either some means to repair the damaged headphones, or else a replacement pair.

My first thought was to go to Guest Relations at the front of the park in City Hall. The Disney cast members there were spectacular. I explained the situation, and they sent for an engineer right away. Shortly thereafter he arrived and we tried to repair the frayed cable, but it turned out the wires were too fine and we weren't going to be able to fix it without solder. Repair was not possible and there was nowhere in the park that sold headphones. I hopped a monorail to the Contemporary Hotel and took a bus from there to Downtown Disney. I had remembered seeing a wall of headphones at the Virgin Megastore there two days earlier. I bought the new headphones, and then bused back to the park.

I caught up with Sara and Ben in Adventureland as they were coming off of Pirates, where Ben had teared up again but not as badly as before. We went on the Jungle Cruise, and as we stood in line Ben put on his new headphones. Sara said he was noticeably calmer now that he had them on. That little side mission had taken me nearly two hours to complete, but it was worth every moment to see Ben smiling and content.

The rest of the day was good — Ben went on Snow White five times that last day, plus at least twice on Peter Pan once it opened. One of the things about the Magic Kingdom is that even on busy days the rides really clear out in the last hour or so as people move back over towards Main Street to watch the fireworks at closing. That means the rides are mostly walk-ons, and Ben took great advantage of that fact. Seeing him communicate where he wanted to go in that last hour, combined with his identifying of the pictures by name on the camera, cemented in my mind that moving there was the right thing to do. I saw Walt Disney World as a massive lever that could move his world and teach him social interaction on a grand scale.

That night in the hotel room Ben saw everyone packing. He was not happy with the idea and kept taking Sara into the bathroom and trying to get her to sit down there so he could run into the other room and unpack. Eventually he grew sleepy, and we finished the last of the packing while he was curled up in bed with his headphones to one side and a big bottle of Pirate Candy to the other.

Our flight home the next day was blessedly uneventful, with Ben either listening to music or watching movies the entire time on the plane. All the way home, my mind alternated between looking forward to seeing Kris, and beginning to plan out how a cross-country move would work. Despite some rough patches, it had been a very successful trip. There was no doubt remaining that we would all be moving to Central Florida before the end of the year.

Chapter 8

Vignettes: Life with an Autistic Child

And so we returned to Seattle and began planning for a cross-country move. I arranged with my company to work remotely full-time, at least on a six-month trial basis. Since I already had the support of my direct manager it turned out to be surprisingly easy to arrange. My relationship with Kris grew day by day. Although I struggled with the thought of what would happen come August, I just kept reminding myself that Kris knew full well what my future plans were. Still, for reasons I will never fully comprehend, she continued to love me. Sara gave her notice at her current school, and began the process of applying for a teaching job in the Orange County Public Schools district in Central Florida. As for Benjamin… well, he continued to be Benjamin.

Ben's expressive language seemed to have stalled at the point of being able to say one simple phrase with a few words substituted as needed. But even though expanding his language remained a battle, actually communicating his wants and needs was less of a problem. Early one Saturday morning he woke up before I did, and decided he was thirsty. He was not able to get his own juice because the huge gallon jug of Gatorade was too large and unwieldy for him to pour. He came into my bedroom to wake me up.

"Juice."

I was sound asleep, and his initial request only elicited a grumble from me.

"Juice."

I began to wake up a little more, but still did not open my eyes. I let out a heavy sigh, and then said, "Ben, you need to ask nicely.

"Daddy, I want juice."

My back was still to him in the darkened room, and I coaxed him further, "No, you need to ask nicely and use all your words."

"Daddy, I want juice. Ok."

At this point I certainly wasn't going to relent until he said please. We had been working on that. He knew very well how to ask politely. So again I prompted him, "Use *all* your words."

Behind me I could hear Ben moving around a little bit. My eyes were still closed, and I could very easily have drifted off back to sleep if Ben were to leave me alone. But Ben was absolutely committed to getting his juice. I heard him fumbling with his mostly-empty juice cup from the night before, and then he lifted one edge of the blanket and pressed the *very cold* juice cup against my bare back, while simultaneously exclaiming, "JUICE!!"

Communication? Not the issue…

Another weekend with Ben and another baffling exchange: it was a lazy Sunday and we were just kind of hanging out in the apartment when Ben looked at me and said, "Daddy, I want some fries. Please."

He asked so nicely, I could hardly say no, right? So into the kitchen I went to heat up a plate of French fries for him to snack on. Fifteen minutes later his afternoon snack was served up and waiting at the dining room table for him. That was the point where he carefully took the plate, set it on the kitchen counter, and then went into the living room and put on his roller skates. "Daddy, I want skating. Please."

He was getting very consistent with his "please" and "thank you", so that was a nice improvement. I was a little confused about this particular order of requests, but I figured we would just go outside and skate for a little while and then come back in later for the fries. Unfortunately Ben then proceeded to pick up the plate of fries, skates still on, and head for the front door. After a few comic circles of me putting down the plate and explaining that we would come back for the fries after we were done skating, followed by Ben picking up the plate again, I finally gave in. He clearly had something specific in mind.

I had to help him down the stairs, and then he skated right over to the car. I opened the door, and he climbed right in, deliriously happy to have the plate of fries in his lap and the skates on his feet. We drove around for a little while and eventually checked out a few used book stores. He was more than happy to change into his regular shoes before going into the stores, and he had long since finished his fries by that point. I am still not sure what that routine was all about, and it was never repeated again.

Another evening with Ben and another baffling exchange: it was getting late in the evening, and for some reason he was becoming progressively more fidgety. Sometimes when he got that way, taking a drive would help calm him down, so I asked him if he wanted to go for a drive. He immediately leapt up, but rather than going to the front door he went to his bedroom instead and put on his pajamas. Okay, I thought, he doesn't want to go out.

Except that as soon as he had his pajamas on, he put on his shoes and socks, a jacket, and then he took me by the hand and led me to the door. Apparently it was "let's drive around in our pajamas" time. Again another mystery, and a particular behavior that he never repeated.

It was a beautiful sunny day in late April, and a rare spring day in the Pacific Northwest. It was actually warm enough for an outdoor swimming pool to be open. Ben had walked with me down to my apartment complex's laundry room so that I could put in a few loads, and then he wanted to go to the playground.

"Daddy, I want *swing*, please!!"

It never got old, hearing him actually talking and making specific requests. It sounded like fun, and so off we went. When we got to the playground we discovered that the pool was open and people were swimming. Ben was absolutely *thrilled*. He dashed into the pool area before I could stop him, took off all of his clothes, and jumped right in. He is surely not cursed with any particular sense of modesty.

The other folks at the pool, including the other kids, were pretty nice about the whole thing. I fished him out, we went back to the apartment to get a towel and some swim trunks, and then went back to the pool. He proceeded to merrily swim for almost two hours, the happiest kid on the planet. The next weekend he spent four hours on Friday and another four hours on Saturday in the swimming pool. I just brought a book and sat by the pool for hours on end while I watched him have the time of his life swimming. I was a little bit shocked that he hadn't actually grown gills by the end of the weekend.

An unusual Wednesday afternoon with Ben in mid-May, and something truly astonishing happened: for the first time ever, I played catch with my son. It sounds like such a trivial thing looking at it in print, but it's not. For the very first time Ben was interested and involved in tossing a ball back and forth with me. He was laughing and smiling each time I would toss the ball to him and he would catch it. At first he would try to carry the ball back to me, but then he picked up on the idea of throwing it back. In the past he had never been interested in any kind of interactive play, anything with give and take. Instead, it has always been about direct stimulation and complete self-containment. The moment that afternoon when he made eye contact with me and looked for me to be ready when he tossed the ball ... *damn*. I was just so proud and happy that I could burst.

Our last few months in Seattle flew by, and at the end of June we also reached the end of the school year and Ben's last day in the classroom at Alternative Elementary 2 (AE2). He had spent the past four years there. Each year the school hosted a picnic after the last day of class for the teachers and families from the classroom. Needless to say, that year was a little weepy. Ben, of course, was completely oblivious; he had a great time playing on the swings and climbing around on the jungle gym, not grasping at all the notion that he would never go back to that classroom. The work that his teachers had done over the previous four years was nothing short of stellar. We had a hard time saying goodbye.

Lisa, his primary teacher, had been teaching at AE2 for five years, her entire teaching career thus far. Her first year in the classroom, Ben was next door in the kindergarten class. He won her heart during his many mad dashes into her room to grab little plastic colored teddy bears from one of her toy bins. By the time he graduated into her classroom, she knew him well. I can honestly say that we could not have asked for a better teacher for Ben. Lisa's patience and skill, her relentless tracking and data collection, and her obvious love of her job and the kids she taught, all combined to make her truly one of the finest teachers I have ever had the pleasure to know. Over those several months, in preparation for our move to Florida, she had gone above and beyond the call of duty not only by compiling all of her data to pass on to the new school district, but also in videotaping Ben in the classroom so that his new teachers would have a clearer understanding of what he was capable, what he was familiar with, and what he had been working towards. I can't even begin to describe how sad I was to see Ben leave her classroom. It would have happened at the start of the next school year anyway, but that did nothing to lessen the pain of not having Lisa as his teacher anymore.

It was equally difficult to say goodbye to Katy and Mark, the two teaching assistants in Ben's classroom. Each had bonded with Ben in different ways, and each had made a measurable impact on his life.

By the end of the picnic there were no dry eyes to be found, and we exchanged lengthy hugs all around. This was it. Nothing left to do but pack up all of our worldly belongings and move to the other side of the country.

Chapter 9

The Big Move

July 24th, 2003 – All of my worldly belongings were loaded into the back of a freight truck, all of my goodbyes were made, and I had two cars to move cross-country. Sara and Ben would remain in Seattle for a few more days before flying to Orlando, staying again at the All Stars. Kris had placed her condo on the market, and would plan her move as soon as that sold. My best friend Riff and I would spend the next eight days driving in tandem across the entire continental United States, each travelling the entire 3,700 miles in separate vehicles.

At the other end of our journey, both Sara and I had already found apartments. Her new home would be directly to the northeast of Disney property, so close that the nightly fireworks at the Magic Kingdom would appear almost right outside her window. I opted for an apartment to the southwest of Disney, just a few miles from the edge of the Animal Kingdom. Each of the apartments would become available on the first of August, and the moving truck would arrive right around the same day.

The cross country drive was nothing short of amazing. Over the course of a week my best friend and I saw the grandeur of the Rocky Mountains as we crossed the Continental Divide in Montana. We spent half a day at Devil's Tower in Wyoming and visited both the Crazy Horse Monument and Mount Rushmore in South Dakota. After seeing the Grand Tetons and the Black Hills, we drove across the long, flat expanse of southern Minnesota.

We spent a fun night hanging out on State Street in Madison, Wisconsin, which reminded me very much of Sixth Street in Austin, Texas or the Ave in Seattle. I guess college towns do tend to be pretty similar. We passed by Chicago, but only at a distance, and then spent two days riding roller coasters at Cedar Point in Sandusky, Ohio. Turning south, we saw a piece of Appalachia as we drove through West Virginia and one small corner of Virginia itself. I honestly think we were in the state of Virginia for a sum total of about ninety minutes.

We began the last day of our drive in Charlotte, North Carolina, passed through South Carolina and Georgia, and just after sunset we finally reached our destination. In seven driving days we had each logged just over 3,700 miles in our two cars, and we were very happy indeed to finally pull into the All Star Movies resort parking lot at Walt Disney World.

We checked into our room, and then I left Riff there to freshen up while I went to see Ben. I knocked on the hotel room door, and when Sara answered I could hear Ben vocalizing inside. As soon as I stepped into the room, Ben got a huge smile on his face, delighted to see me. Then he suddenly realized that he was mad at me for disappearing for over a week. He proceeded to spend the next fifteen minutes pointedly avoiding me, while still glancing over and smiling any time he thought I wasn't looking. It was really great to see him.

The next morning I signed the lease on my new apartment and carried up the car load of stuff that had made the trek with me across North America. Because the truck with all my furniture wasn't going to arrive for several more days, I bought a couple of air mattresses for Riff and me to sleep on in the interim. I spent the afternoon hanging out with Ben at the Magic Kingdom so that Sara could sign *her* lease and begin to settle into her own new place. It was so nice spending the afternoon with him after all of the days and days of driving, to finally get some of the hugs and kisses I had been craving from him the night before.

I also spent the next day with Ben, initially bringing him over to my new apartment so that he could see it. He really liked it, especially the inflatable mattresses which he thought were really funny.

In the early afternoon I experienced my first real Florida thunderstorm, and it was a doozy! Afternoon thunderstorms are common in Florida in the summer, showing up like clockwork so they can be planned around. This one, though, was particularly strong.

Lightning strikes happened all around us, and I think one of them struck the local cell tower because I lost all cell service in my area for several hours. Just a few miles away an apartment building was hit directly, sparking a fire that destroyed four apartment units. At my building one of the nearby strikes triggered the building alarm, which was a piercing whine that was absolutely unbearable. It was so bad that I had to take Ben out onto the breezeway outside the apartment to escape the noise, and then when it became obvious the alarm was not going to be shut off anytime soon I took him down to sit in the car. With the rain coming down in sheets I didn't really want to drive anywhere, but at least it was cool and sheltered. Oddly enough, Ben was not particularly bothered by the storm. He watched the water flowing down across the windshield and listened to the booming thunder along with the constant drumming of rain on the car's roof, and seemed to think it was an interesting spectacle.

Being from Seattle, I thought I knew all about rain, but I had never experienced anything like that before. Aside from the incredible fury of the storm, the oddest thing to me was that my brain automatically equated a gray, overcast and rainy day to be *chilly*, whereas in Florida it was almost unbearably warm. It would take me a good long while to get used to that.

Once the rain slackened a bit, Ben and I went for a drive to explore the area. I had only been there once briefly in February when I scouted out the apartment, and I had not taken the time to see the neighborhood at all. Ben was just as interested in exploring as I was, and we began to get a general idea of where things were. A few hours later we met up with Sara at the gates of the Magic Kingdom. It was still raining, but Ben was undaunted and led us directly to Snow White's Scary Adventures for several more rides as well as a spin around Peter Pan's Flight.

By the time we finished that ride the nightly fireworks show was starting. In the past Ben had wanted to have nothing to do with the fireworks, preferring to get as far away as possible. This time he actually stopped dead in his tracks and was watching with a big smile on his face. Once the show was over he went with his mom back to their hotel room while I linked up with Riff. It turns out Riff had been at the Animal Kingdom during the storm, out on the safari tour during the worst of it. He said it was absolutely amazing to be out on the African plains amidst all the animals during the full fury of the storm. He didn't mind at all the fact that he had gotten completely drenched. We went back home (home!) so that Riff could dry off and then we got some sleep.

On the fourth of August the moving truck finally arrived, and we spent the entire day unloading two households. First we had to unload all of Sara's things out of the big truck and into her new apartment. Then we had to unload all of *my* things out of the big truck, onto a U-Haul, drive that over to my apartment, and finally unload everything there. Fortunately we had a moving crew to help, but even so it made for a very long day.

Of course I still had a ton of unpacking to do, but my new home was finally starting to feel like a *home*. Sara and Ben were settling into their new home as well, and all was right with the world.

I had one more lazy day after that to hang out with my friend at Disney World. Then, with great sadness, it was time to take Riff to the airport and send him on his way with a hearty thanks for all of his help in the previous two weeks. The chaos of the move was finally over, and it was time to start settling into my new life in Florida.

Once settled into our new homes, our first order of business was to get Ben enrolled in the local school district. There was much paperwork to be done. Ben's initial school assignment was rapidly changed to a different elementary school. It was a little further away but had an autism program. The school itself was beautiful, only a year old and located in one of the wealthier parts of town. We met his new teacher, as well as the classroom assistants. We were very pleased with what we saw.

Although Ben was not exactly thrilled with having to get up early in the morning and go back to school, his first day back was uneventful. His teacher was nice enough to call about halfway through the school day to let Sara know that Ben was doing just fine. He had settled right into the routine and recognized the tasks that he was being asked to do in the classroom. When the bus dropped him off at home in the afternoon he was in a very good mood (if a little tired and shell-shocked from the day). He proceeded to cocoon himself in his play room, watching tapes, eating fries, and just generally reassuring himself that everything was okay.

Around the same time, Sara was interviewed and then ultimately offered a job teaching English at a local high school. By late August, we were finally settled into a pretty standard routine. I would come to Sara's place in the morning to get Ben ready for school while she left for work. I would get Ben safely on the bus before returning to my new home office to get to work. Sara would get home from work in time to get Ben off the bus. Since school let out an hour earlier on Wednesdays, I would get Ben off the bus and take him to the Magic Kingdom. Sara would meet us for some fries at Cosmic Ray's, and then we would spend a few hours in Fantasyland. On the weekend, Ben and I would go to the park at least once, if not twice.

I had mentally kept a running count of how many times Ben had ridden Snow White's Scary Adventures, and it was around this time that I started actually keeping the definite tally in my journal.

On the whole, Ben seemed very happy with the move. It took about two weeks for him to really begin to settle into his new home(s), but by early September he was successfully sleeping through the night in his own bed. The routine of school played into his need for predictable patterns, the time spent at Disney offered abundant opportunities for working on socialization and life skills. He certainly enjoyed all of the sunshine.

For my part, I felt like I was sleepwalking through most of my days. When I was with Ben I felt alive, but the rest of the time I mostly sat alone in my apartment. I worked crazy hours, partially because the people I worked with were three hours behind me and partially because I just didn't have anything better to do. Without Kris there, my home just felt empty. I looked forward to our regular phone conversations, and counted the days until her first trip down to visit me.

Interlude

The Proposal

Here's the story about Kris' first visit:

I had already decided more than a month earlier that I was going to propose to Kris the first time she came down. The simple truth was, I just did not feel right about asking her to uproot her entire life, sell her home, leave her family, and move to the opposite corner of the country without a real commitment from me. She deserved better than that (although I still did not quite understand why she was settling for me). With all of the pandemonium of the move, I had no way to propose before I left. I wanted it to be a special moment. I instead plotted how to pop the question to her at the Magic Kingdom without giving away the surprise.

And so it was that on the nineteenth of September, 2003, I took Kris on her first visit to Walt Disney World. We had a very lovely day walking around the Magic Kingdom. I went out of my way to play the tour guide pointing out little details here and there. I think Kris fully expected me to propose to her that day since she tensed up every time we passed any kind of romantic location with a scenic view of Cinderella Castle. Of course, I did not want to be that predictable. I had something more obscure in mind to catch her off guard.

We had been on several rides that day, and by early afternoon we reached the Haunted Mansion. I explained to her how, although it seems like there is no real story to the ride, there really is a through-line about The Bride and her doomed marriage to the man who would eventually become the Ghost Host that narrates the attraction. I showed her all the little hints and details in the decorations, both in the line and on the ride itself.

As we exited the building I walked her to a specific spot in the pavement and told her the story of how the Groom, completely distraught after his Bride's untimely death, had thrown her wedding ring out the window only to have it land embedded in the pavement below. In order to show her the exact place, I got down on one knee and pointed to the ring that was plainly visible in the ground at the edge of the gates (although it has since been removed, which is a real shame). Prior to kneeling down, I palmed the real engagement ring, and as I looked up into her eyes I simply said, "…and speaking of rings…"

Kris nearly fainted on the spot. She grew weak in the knees, and kind of stumbled over to a nearby low wall where she could sit, hyperventilating.

"So, umm… was that a yes?"

"Yes!" she exclaimed, "of course yes!!"

Chapter 10

Life in Florida

Kris' visit ended much too soon, and life continued on with the same pattern. As the summer crowds faded completely away and Disney went into its late fall lull, it became easier for Ben to go on multiple rides on Snow White's Scary Adventures. I tragically learned that it was actually possible to complete six laps in eighteen minutes, and it was not unusual for Ben to go on it 20-25 times in a single day.

His mother and I both became concerned about this obsession. It was a tricky problem. On the one hand, this was the world's largest carrot we could possibly dangle in front of him. We were definitely able to use other areas of the park as practical lessons in real world life skills. On the other hand, the obsession threatened to overwhelm everything else we were trying to accomplish by taking him there.

Eventually we came up with some very specific ground rules. Ben could go on the ride, but after completing a lap he would have to leave the ride area entirely and walk to the nearby gift shop where we required him to use all of his words and ask nicely to go again. "Mama/Daddy, I want more Snow White, please!" On top of that we would only allow him to go three times before he had to go do something else. This seemed like a happy medium, keeping him interested and engaged while forcing him to expand his interests and spend time in other areas of the park.

Occasionally I would attempt to take him to other Disney parks, with varying success. On one Sunday I was feeling somehow reluctant to go back to the Magic Kingdom for the third day in a row, having myself ridden Snow White's Scary Adventures more than twenty times in the previous 48 hours. On a whim I tried taking Ben to the Disney MGM Studios instead. I had to physically drag him out of the car. All the way to the tram he tried to pull me back to the car while complaining loudly. As we sat down on the tram he started making his normal "frustrated" sounds (something like, "ya ya ho HHEEEEHHHHGGGG!" and "ke to has to HEHHHiieeaAAAHHH!!"), and then climbed into my lap, gave me a pleading stare, and said, "Daddy, I want CAR!"

Reluctantly we gave up on Disney/MGM. From there I headed over to Epcot expecting more of the same but willing to at least give it a try. When we parked he wasn't exactly eager to get out of the car, but he wasn't fighting it either. As we walked towards the entrance he would stop every twenty or thirty feet to look up at Spaceship Earth, all the while screening it with his left hand kind of like the "I'm crushing your head" guy from *The Kids in the Hall*.

Then he started one of his conversations with me, which went something like:

Ben: "Fun."

Me: "Fun"

Ben: "Fuffin."

Me: "Fuffin."

Ben: "And a-goofin' "

Me: "And a-goofin' "

Ben: "And I go fuffin."

Me: "And I go fuffin."

I have no idea what it means, but we have that conversation often.

As we walked and talked, he got a smile on his face and even started skipping. We went through the turnstiles and for the first time since we moved to Florida in August, Ben was actually in a different Disney park than the Magic Kingdom. Yay!

We went on Spaceship Earth, which lasts a little over 20 minutes. Ben loved the whole thing, turning and looking around at everything. Not surprisingly, his favorite part was when a large video screen displayed the scene from *Snow White* with the dwarfs dancing and singing to "The Silly Song".

After Spaceship Earth, he led me over towards the side of Future World with The Living Seas and The Land, but changed his mind and decided to explore a garden path instead. Then we meandered over towards the World Showcase, but again he changed his mind as we neared Mexico. I assured him that I wasn't going to take him on any scary rides, but he still didn't want to walk that way. I didn't want to push it, because I wanted him to enjoy being in the park even if he wasn't ready to explore very far.

Instead of going to the World Showcase, we stayed in Future World and wound up walking back by Test Track and then the Mission: Space plaza. Because we were right there, I took him into the Mission: Space gift shop to see what he would think of it. He wandered into the Mission: Space Race training area, which had a huge collaborative game and also a plethora of interactive side exhibits. One of the areas was a climbing play area, kind of like the ones at McDonald's but with a space theme. He was thrilled! He played and climbed around in there for almost an hour. At one point he even sent a video postcard to his grandma (I did all the typing, but he picked the background and posed for the camera).

We next spent some time in the Wonders of Life pavilion, and a good long time in the Mouse Gear gift shop and the Art of Disney store. All total we spent nearly three hours in Epcot, and for most of that time he was smiling and skipping. This was a definite victory.

Another victory happened one Wednesday in November while Ben was at the Magic Kingdom with his mother. I will warn you that this particular victory falls into the category of "scatological parental pride", so anyone that gets grossed out by that kind of thing might want to skip the next paragraph.

While at the park that afternoon, Ben pooped in the toilet for the very first time. At ten years old he was still nowhere near potty trained, and continued to wear pull-ups everywhere. He had begun making progress at urinating in the toilet and was usually staying dry for much of the day, but this was the very first time he had ever actually defecated in the toilet. He and Sara had just finished riding the Tomorrowland Transit Authority and were walking from Tomorrowland back over to Fantasyland when he started doing that leg-crossing thing. Sara took him to the nearest restroom. Needless to say, she was quite literally floored when he proceeded to do his business. We were still a long way from getting rid of diapers, but it was a huge first step and I was absolutely thrilled when Sara called to tell me about it.

Even after ten years of living with this autistic child, Ben would still manage to find ways to surprise and perplex me. Around the beginning of January of 2004 he picked up a new hobby: kicking his own butt. It took a little effort, but for some mysterious reason he figured out how to do it. He would get a running start taking long strides, and then let his right leg swing back completely with his knee totally bent so that his right heel would hit his backside.

The first time I saw him do that, I thought to myself, "Now that's a sight to behold…"

I supposed that life would be a lot easier if Ben was like other kids, but then again it would be a heck of a lot less interesting.

Winter turned to spring, and in April of 2004 we encountered our first real challenge: Snow White's Scary Adventures was scheduled to be closed for over a month for a complete rehab. Needless to say, we were worried about how Ben would react. As a matter of fact, one of the regular Disney cast members who worked the ride and had gotten to know Ben was equally concerned. She actually went to her supervisor to get special permission so she could walk the entire ride path one night after closing and take extensive pictures from start to finish. She presented those pictures to us just before the ride closed, and I put them into a photo album for Ben to carry around and look at during that month. As it turns out, that is an album that he still carries with him to this day.

On his first visit to the park with Snow White closed, Ben was very confused when he came around the corner and saw that a blue construction wall had been erected in front of the ride. I had expected that he would throw a fit but was pleasantly surprised. I gave him the new picture book, and he sat and paged through it for about fifteen minutes. After a while he was ready to go try something else. We wound up going on a bunch of stuff he hadn't done in quite a while. Winnie the Pooh, Dumbo, Tomorrowland Transit Authority, Buzz Lightyear, Mickey's PhilharMagic ... he had a great evening and was very happy the whole time. Every now and then he would stop and look at his Snow White pictures for a while, but he never really got upset.

The next visit did not go quite as well.

He came home from school already talking about the Magic Kingdom, and he went into his room and grabbed the die cast metal replica of the Snow White mine cart that I had gotten him for Christmas. Uh-oh.

He had his usual Wednesday dinner at Cosmic Ray's and then made a bee line for Snow White. He was ... *less than understanding* when he discovered it was still closed. He tried to force open the construction wall. He opened up both of his picture books and repeatedly pointed at the pictures of Snow White.

"I want Snow White, please! Go there!!"

I kept trying to calm him down explaining that Snow White was still closed and would he like to go see Pooh instead?

"F***ING!!"

Now that's a doozy of a word for him to have learned. I can't exactly say I was thrilled to hear him scream it in public for the entire world to hear, especially in the middle of Fantasyland in the Magic Kingdom. On the upside, at least he was definitely using a new word correctly in context. That's progress, right?

After a while we convinced him to leave the ride and get some candy. Following a trip to the Main Street Confectionary he went to Exposition Hall to watch cartoons in the theater for a while. He sat all the way through "The Band Concert" and most of the way through "Steamboat Willie" before he was ready to leave. We were just walking under the Main Street train station towards the park's exit when he started frantically looking through his backpack. I asked him what he was trying to find, and he looked me straight in the eye and said, "Skittles, please."

Sure enough, he had dropped his bag of candy back in the theater. I ran back and found it, and upon returning it to him he was perfectly happy. On the monorail he was smiling and laughing. By the time we got back to the car he was as happy as could be. So all in all the day wasn't a failure, and I think under the circumstances he actually handled his frustration pretty dang well aside from the one outburst.

Much to Ben's relief, the four weeks of rehab finally passed and the ride reopened on a bright Monday in May. I even called the park that morning to confirm it was open since I did not want to tell Ben it was back only to disappoint him. Sara picked him up from school that day, and I met them at the gates to the Magic Kingdom. Ben was equal parts excited and apprehensive, marching directly up Main Street with confidence and purpose. As he entered Fantasyland he started to slow down, obviously afraid it was all a cruel joke and he was going to come around the corner and be greeted by a big blue construction wall like last time. When he came around the bend by Sir Mickey's he briefly stumbled in surprise and then *ran* to get in line for his favorite ride. He was a little concerned because the layout of the line had changed to accommodate new control panels, but once he was on the ride itself he was grinning ear to ear.

As excited as he was, though, he did his normal three laps around Snow White and then he was ready to go. Being in the park on a Monday was just too weird for him, but he was obviously contented to know that his ride was safe and sound. At that moment I'd say he was the happiest kid on the planet.

Not long after that, Kris finally got an offer on her condo. After living three thousand miles apart for almost a year, she was at last able to move down to Florida that July. Her timing was impeccable, in that she arrived just in time to experience Hurricane Charley, Hurricane Francis, Hurricane Ivan, and Hurricane Jeanne all within a single month. I had reassured her the year before that we never, ever got hurricanes because our location in Central Florida was so far inland, and she had nothing to worry about. Now here it was, her second month of living in Florida, and four different hurricanes walked directly over our location within the space of twenty seven days.

We weathered the storms to no ill effect, and whatever power outages we experienced were fairly brief, only a matter of hours in fact. Ben did not seem troubled at all by the weather, he just kind of shrugged his shoulders and either watched videos on the TV if there was power or else on the laptop computer if there was not.

The rest of the year passed uneventfully. We were still going to the Magic Kingdom two or three times per week. By the end of 2004 Ben was up to 900 times on the ride. I began to think about what we might do for Ben's 1,000th ride, which we had all begun referring to as SW1K. Being a software developer, I had been involved in the whole Y2K (Year 2000) furor four years earlier, and the naming shorthand stuck in my head. Regarding SW1K I had in mind some kind of simple family celebration, but what Disney came up with turned out to be just a bit more.

Chapter 11

SW1K

On the second weekend of April, 2005, Ben rode Snow White's Scary Adventures 33 times, bringing his running total to 987 and effectively ensuring that the next weekend would see his 1,000th ride. Everybody was very excited about this but Ben, who really didn't seem to attach any particular significance to the number of rides. Honestly, the only reason we had an accurate count was my own personal obsession. I had been keeping a running tally in my journal. I had also posted occasionally about Ben on the forums of the popular unofficial Disney website WDWMagic.com. Several people on that forum had suggested ideas on how to commemorate SW1K. The one that I really liked was seeing if we could actually get Snow White to go on the ride with Ben.

I tried calling Disney Guest Services, and was essentially told to check in with them when we got to the park that day and they would see what they could do. That was not a very reassuring stance on which to hang my hat. But when I posted my dilemma on the WDWMagic board, I was immediately contacted by someone who knew the stage manager of the Cinderellabration show, which features Snow White and which performs throughout the day at the Magic Kingdom.

The biggest concern was that, from a legal standpoint, Disney generally does not allow costumed characters to go inside dark rides because of the potential liability. Much remained up in the air right until late the night before the big day when I received a phone call from Graham Murphy, the afore-mentioned stage manager. Graham was able to arrange a personal meet and greet for Ben with Snow White immediately following the 11:40 a.m. performance of Cinderellabration. After a short visit she would personally escort Ben to her ride and join him for his 1,000th trip. Needless to say, we were all very excited, except for Ben, who was sound asleep at that point.

Saturday morning, April 16th: Usually I don't take Ben to the Magic Kingdom until the afternoon, but because we had a commitment to meet Snow White at noon and because Ben still had a few more trips to get under his belt prior to the big 1,000, we left for the park just after 9:30 in the morning. Going that much earlier in the day presented several problems. First of all, it was just generally an unusual thing to do, and Ben is always thrown off-kilter by unusual changes in routine. The next, more serious complication, was that Ben wanted to stop for fries, but all of the typical fast food burger joints are still serving breakfast at that time of the morning, so no fries were available. From Ben's perspective, I was dragging him out of the house at a weird time and then refusing to even provide him with sustenance. He was understandably upset and cranking up steadily. I knew if I let it continue to build that it was going to throw him off for the entire day. Fortunately I had a secret weapon stashed in the back seat of my car: Pirate Candy.

The very same candy that he had discovered on our very first trip to Orlando three years earlier had always worked as sort of a magic talisman to calm Ben down and make him happy. At ten bucks a pop it's not a talisman that can be whipped out on a regular basis, but it just so happened that I had made a special trip to the Magic Kingdom the day before to get one for him as a surprise. I had intended to give it to him for the 1,000th ride, but it was obvious that I was going to have to spring it on him earlier than that.

At first when I reached behind his seat and pulled out the bottle his response was essentially, "I want fries, you idiot, not some stupid bottle of candy!!" He took it out of my hand, stuffed it into the front pocket of his backpack sitting on the floor in front of him, and continued to complain. Then, like something out of a Bugs Bunny cartoon, his complaints slowly tapered off and he took on that facial expression of, "...hey... wait a minute...." He looked down at the bottle, and then got a big smile on his face and snatched it up. The immediate crisis had been defused.

The next hurdle became obvious as we approached the entrance to the Magic Kingdom parking lot. With our typical pattern of arriving at the park around two in the afternoon, we were always part of a trickle of cars drifting into the park. No big deal. But arriving at the park within an hour of opening, we were part of the mass migration into the most heavily attended theme park, as well as the fourth largest parking lot, in the world. It had been a very long time since either of us had been a part of that chaos, and honestly we were *both* a little thrown.

We were parked in the Daisy section of the parking lot, the furthest back on the west side. In the time it took us to walk from the car to the tram loading spot, the entire lot was filled and cars had already filled up more than half of the next section that had opened up. There was no sign of them slowing down. The standing crowd was too large for us to make it on the first tram, so we had to wait for the next one to come along. Me, I was worried about how it was going to take substantially longer to get into the park than usual and worried that Ben was going to be completely overwhelmed by the crowds and the noise. Then I glanced down at Ben, who sat calmly on the tram holding his bottle of pirate candy and smiling in anticipation of going on his favorite ride. Go figure.

The trip on the monorail was uneventful, aside from being much more crowded than it usually was when we arrived in the afternoons. We pulled into the Magic Kingdom station and Ben literally leapt out of his seat to head out to the Magic Kingdom gates. Passing through security and the turnstiles was a breeze. (I am constantly amazed at just how good Disney is at moving very large numbers of people very efficiently. They should contract out to the people who run airports). Ben hit Main Street briskly, with a real bounce in his step, and we were off to the races!

Across the hub at the bottom of Main Street, into the Main Street Confectionary, through the two adjacent gift shops, and then back onto the street. Threading through the outside of the main Hub at the top of Main Street, deftly avoiding the crowd of people watching the morning's first performance of Cinderellabration in front of the castle, take the quiet side path past the rose garden, then across the walkway towards Cosmic Ray's with a quick hard left at the last moment to follow the pathway past the Wishing Well and up into the courtyard behind the castle. A quick stop in front of Sir Mickey's to sit down on his favorite bench, and then he was on to his first ride of the day on Snow White's Scary Adventures.

Because we were seriously behind schedule and had less than an hour before we were supposed to meet up with Graham, I allowed Ben to do five straight laps on the ride instead of the usual three.

Somewhere around the third or fourth lap Kris arrived to join in on the festivities. It was after the fifth ride that Ben said the word that struck terror into my heart: "Monorail." After only five rides, and with less than a half hour until he was scheduled to meet Snow White in person, he was ready to leave the park. Oh crap.

Ben led us back down the pathway past the Wishing Well, and as we emerged in front of Cosmic Ray's I quickly convinced him that we should go in and get some fries. He thought about it for a second, and then grudgingly agreed. Crisis temporarily averted.

Twenty minutes later, after devouring his order of fries, we were once again headed back to Fantasyland and another two rides on SWSA. We were still six rides short of where we needed to be, but at that point I was resigned to slightly fudging the numbers for the sake of decorum. It was time to meet up with Graham and go meet Snow White in person.

I have to say that Graham was every bit as good a guy in person as he had seemed on the phone. He was the epitome of the Disney cast member, friendly and outgoing, and doing everything he can to create a magical experience for the guest. The work he did on Ben's behalf was something that meant the world to me. He got a well-deserved personal thank you letter from me a few days later.

Graham took us over to the castle breezeway where we would wait for Snow White to emerge. Around this time Ryland and Corinne, two other members from the WDWMagic board, arrived to shoot video of the event. Sara was still nowhere to be seen. I worried that she was going to miss out on the big event, but there was nothing to be done about it. I had no way of reaching her, and no idea what was delaying her arrival.

Ben was getting antsy and asking to go take a monorail. I was squatted down on the floor with Ben sitting on my knee, talking quietly to him and telling him how good he was being, and that he just needed to wait a little bit longer. I had my back to the door from which Snow White emerged, but I still knew it the moment that she appeared: Ben suddenly went rigid, stopped breathing, and became absolutely silent. Imagine the person you most respect and admire in the world, and then imagine that this person suddenly appeared in front of you. Ben was awestruck.

Snow White walked right up to Ben and said hello, telling him how happy she was to meet him. Ben finally took a breath. When she knelt down and opened her arms, Ben leaned right in and gave her a big hug.

Awestruck

Most of that visit was a blur to me. There was just so much happening so quickly. I remember Ben being completely overwhelmed (but in a good way). I remember Kris taking pictures while other people where shooting video, and then Snow White asked Ben if he would like to go see her ride. Ben took off like a shot towards Snow White's Scary Adventures, and I had to physically slow him down to get him to wait for the princess to keep up.

We got to the ride, and the crowd in line let out a collective gasp. Children were pointing, calling out "Mommy! Mommy! It's really Snow White!!" Ben was escorted directly to the front of the line, and then sat in the front row of the mine cart. Snow White sat down right next to him, and began pointing out things in the giant mural on the wall next to them. Ben was squirming in his seat. To someone who didn't know him, he probably seemed very uncomfortable. What I saw in him was that he was simply beside himself, unable to believe what was happening. He studiously avoided making eye contact with her, but he kept giving her sly little sideways glances whenever he thought she might not be looking. I sat in the row directly behind them, with Graham next to me. Sitting in the back row were Ryland and Corinne, filming the whole thing. Kris stayed behind so she could take pictures as we emerged at the end of the ride.

Throughout the ride, Snow White kept talking to Ben about everything that was going on while Ben kept studiously looking at everything except her. Of all the hundreds upon hundreds of trips through Snow White's Scary Adventures that I had gone on with Ben, that was by far the most magical. Soon enough the ride ended, and Kris was there to snap a photo of Ben and Snow White emerging through the final doorway.

Upon exiting the ride vehicle, Snow White stayed to talk to Ben for a few minutes longer until it was time for her to leave to prepare for her next performance at Cinderellabration. As she was about to leave, she said goodbye to Ben and blew him a little kiss. He immediately blew a kiss right back at her, and then turned and sprinted to get back on the ride for another trip. I thanked Graham and Snow White profusely and then dashed over to catch up with Ben.

Not Really SW1K

He did another two laps on the ride, probably because he always did three in a row and needed to finish that pattern. It was right about then that Sara finally showed up. She was in tears, completely distraught about missing the big event. Apparently she had grabbed the wrong pass when she went out the door, and although she arrived at the park early she was unable to get through the turnstiles because she didn't have a valid pass. She had begged and pleaded with Guest Services, explaining what was happening, and they finally were able to verify her identity and that she had a valid pass and let her through the turnstiles. Unfortunately, she had been delayed just long enough to miss the entire thing.

Ben was happy to see her but was still tremendously overwhelmed by everything that had happened. He made it very clear that he was ready to go. He wanted to go take a monorail. The four of us (Ben, Sara, Kris and I) worked our way back towards Main Street and then back down to the Main Street Confectionary. It was there that something very unusual happened. Normally Ben would stop there on the way out of the park, pick out some candy, and then we would go. This time he walked through the shop and then found a quiet little niche at the front of the store in a bay of windows that looked out onto the town square. He sat there with Sara for a good ten or fifteen minutes, just kind of decompressing. The events of the past hour were really quite a lot for him to digest, and he needed a little quiet time to get his legs back under him.

Then he seemed to decide that hey, we didn't really need to leave after all. He led us all in a little parade right back up to Fantasyland. Eight more rides on Snow White's Scary Adventures, interspersed with rides on Small World and Peter Pan, and he spent a total of nearly five hours in the park.

It seemed only right that Sara should ride alone with him for the actual 1,000th ride, which I suppose was a small consolation but at least it was something. Ben was dog tired, and truthfully so was I. We all dragged ourselves home and spent the rest of the evening more or less on autopilot. Ben was sound asleep by 9pm and slept like a rock all night long.

The Real SW1K

The week after the big event, Ben and I were in the park when we were stopped by one of the regular cast members we would often see. She asked when Ben was going to hit the big 1,000. I told her it had already happened and how it went off, but she said that the Fantasyland cast members still wanted to do something special for Ben. She asked for my phone number and told me to expect a call in the next few days.

A week later I received a call from the manager in charge of Fantasyland. He told me that all of the people in Fantasyland were very excited to hear about Ben's achievement. And they wanted to do something special for him. We agreed that Ben would stop by City Hall on Main Street the next Saturday at 1:30 for a special treat.

That weekend we arrived at City Hall to introduce ourselves and were quickly escorted into a private room where Snow White, Dopey, and three of our favorite regular cast members were waiting to greet us. Many pictures were taken, and many gifts were given. Snow White presented Ben with a prince's crown and then a certificate to commemorate his 1,000 rides. Then Dopey presented Ben with a bag of pixie dust. When shown the dust, Ben very carefully put it back into the pouch for safe keeping. They also gave Ben a very nice picture frame to put his SW1K photo in.

Lastly, they gave him a genuine Walt Disney World cast member nametag. It was one of the brand new ones with the "Happiest Celebration on Earth" theme, and with Benjamin's name proudly engraved on it. For anyone not familiar with how important the nametags are, *this is a big deal*. During the course of the afternoon Ben was stopped by at least a dozen cast members, asking how he got a real nametag. One cast member pointed out that having a real nametag meant that Benjamin was allowed to go backstage, although we never attempted that particular feat. That nametag was such a big deal that later that day on the way out of the park, when Ben sat down on a bench to rest for a bit, we were approached by a very large, solid, security-looking cast member who very politely shook us down to find out why Ben had a real nametag. When I explained that it was a gift from the Fantasyland cast members to commemorate his riding Snow White's Scary Adventures over a thousand times, he seemed more than a little surprised. First he was surprised that a cast member would make that gift, but then we could see the number click in his head and he asked, "How many times did you say?" When I replied that as of that day he had been on the ride 1,036 times, all he could say was "Wow ... "

After Ben was given all of his presents, he of course made off like a shot to go on his ride. After only going around twice, he had the same delayed response that he had back on the 16th — he asked to go take a monorail and go home. We got back to the Main Street Confectionary where he chilled out in his favorite little quiet bay window, and after about fifteen minutes he was ready to spend more time in the park.

We took the train from Main Street around to Frontierland and then walked over to watch the big drop at Splash Mountain. We promptly left after the first big splash. From there we strolled up through Frontierland and Liberty Square, looked at flag-themed shirts in the Heritage House for a few minutes, and then got some lunch at the Columbia Harbour House. From that point it was a fairly typical Saturday afternoon at the Magic Kingdom for Ben, with a total of eleven rides on Snow White's Scary Adventures plus rides on The Many Adventures of Winnie the Pooh, Mickey's PhilharMagic, the Tomorrowland Transit Authority, and Buzz Lightyear. We spent a total of 4 1/2 hours in the park, and a grand time was had by all.

Ben went to sleep that night holding his new picture frame with the SW1K picture in it and with a contented smile on his face. I swear, I think he'd marry that girl.

Chapter 12

The Good Times and the Bad

A few months after the excitement of SW1K, another very exciting event took place. Exactly two years to the day after I got in my car and began the drive to Orlando for the big move, on July 24th of 2005, Kris and I got married. We had kind of a guerilla ceremony, taking place at Cinderella's Wishing Well in the shadow of Cinderella Castle and done completely without Disney's blessing.

Our wedding party was tiny. Aside from Kris and me the party included my best friend Riff, who officiated the wedding after going online and becoming ordained through the Universal Life Church; my mom, whom I had moved to Florida as well so that I could care for her; two friends of Kris' from Tampa; and Corinne and Ryland, the two friends who had filmed the SW1K event for us and graciously offered to also film our wedding.

The ceremony itself was extremely brief. Neither Kris nor I was interested in a big to-do. Right before the wedding we ducked into the restrooms at Cosmic Ray's restaurant in Tomorrowland and changed into our wedding attire, which for me consisted of a nice black and white guayabera and some nice black long shorts, and for Kris consisted of a lovely, simple white dress. As for Riff, he dressed the part in white slacks and a black shirt complete with steel collar tips and a white preacher's collar. Once dressed, our party of eight converged on the Wishing Well. As we were arranging ourselves a Kodak photographer happened to walk by and asked us what was up. The Kodak photographers wander around the Disney parks with professional cameras and offer to take high quality pictures for park guests at no up-front cost. Upon hearing we were getting married he offered to stay and take photos, to which we readily agreed. The entire ceremony lasted well under fifteen minutes and was exactly what we had hoped for – simple, meaningful, and brief. We said our vows, kissed, and then the photographer took a lovely photo of us holding hands over the wishing well with Cinderella Castle in the background. He then gave us a little plastic card with a code on it so that we could go online later to view the pictures and purchase prints if we liked them.

Once the ceremony was over, Kris changed out of her dress and into more comfortable clothes, and then we spent the remainder of the day touring the Magic Kingdom and Epcot while proudly wearing our new bride and groom mouse ear hats. The bride's version was white with a veil while the groom's was a black top hat. While at Epcot we were even invited by a cast member to view the IllumiNations fireworks show from a private vantage point in the England pavilion where our group could stand right at the stone wall and view the entire show with a perfect, unobstructed view.

It was a lovely end to a lovely day. That night Kris and I stayed at a nearby hotel, before catching a flight the next morning for our honeymoon in New York City. Life was very, very good.

That same summer, Ben successfully completed his last year in grade school, so when August rolled around he was ready to begin classes as a Middle School student. Unfortunately, where we had found public schools to be perfectly suited for Ben at the grade school level, we soon discovered that the middle school experience was entirely different. Ben was miserable there, did not like his teachers at all, and spent a great deal of time trying to escape. Since his classroom happened to be right on the bus loop, on more than one occasion he even attempted to climb out the classroom window and make a run for the street in front of the school.

To make matters worse, his behavior was also rapidly going downhill. One day at school he actually hit his teacher in the face with a video tape. He also became increasingly aggressive towards his classmates, hitting them at every opportunity. His behavior at home was equally problematic. One evening he head butted his mother in the nose when she refused to take him to Wal-Mart.

Even at Disney it was becoming a serious issue. On more than one occasion I had to bodily carry him out of the park in order to prevent him from potentially injuring other guests. He had learned that hitting us would not elicit the desired response. As a result, when he got upset he would start randomly hitting or kicking passing strangers. It is not much fun to juggle physically restraining your child while simultaneously apologizing to the innocent bystander who just got kicked in the shin without warning.

Along with the violent outbursts, his sleep patterns once again had become a huge issue. One night in particular he was so agitated and opposed to sleep that at 4:30am I was forced to throw all the breaker switches in my apartment's breaker box because the only way to stop him from turning on lights and electronics was to cut all power to the living room, dining room, hallway, and bedroom. Even so, it was nearly 5:30am before he finally fell asleep. Something had to change, and soon, for the sake of my family's sanity.

We took him to his primary doctor, an autism specialist, who suggested a new medication in order to reduce Ben's anxiety. Theoretically the new meds should not have had any serious side effects, but within a few days of starting them, Ben would projectile vomit whenever he took a dose. After having that joyous experience a couple of times we had no choice but to switch back to his previous medications and look for other solutions.

In the midst of all of this turmoil, as 2005 slowly wound to a close, I received an interesting email from Len Testa, one of the authors of the very excellent *Unofficial Guide to Walt Disney World*. He had heard about Ben's Snow White fixation and wanted to meet him. I thought it would be cool to meet someone behind the book that made our first visits to WDW survivable, so of course I agreed.

Ben and I arrived at the Magic Kingdom parking lot bright and early at 9am on the day of our meeting, and Sara met us at the Ticket and Transportation Center. From there we took the monorail around to the Magic Kingdom where we walked right into the filming of the Christmas Day Parade for ABC. They film for several days early in December and then edit it together for the broadcast.

Long before then we had discovered the Guest Assistance Pass (GAP) that Disney provides for any park guests requiring special accommodations. Since we live locally, they will usually write the pass to be good for three months, and Ben's GAP had expired since our previous visit. After stopping by City Hall to renew Ben's GAP, we then worked our way through the crowd on Main Street. Ben was a little chagrinned at not being able to cross over to the other side of the street because of the filming, but all in all he was cool about it.

The crowds and the filming equipment forced us to take a circuitous path to get to Fantasyland, and soon enough Ben was making his first run on Snow White's Scary Adventures. After getting off the first time we noticed a group of four people who looked like they were waiting for someone, so I went over and asked if one of them was Len. Sure enough it was him and three other people from the Guide.

They were all very excited to meet Ben and came bearing gifts. They gave us an autographed copy of the new 2006 edition of the Guide, a baseball cap, several collector's pins including one that Len described as the original prototype pin (the first test shot before manufacturing), and a Touring Plan t-shirt autographed by a bunch of people both from the Guide and from major unofficial Disney websites like Jim Hill Media, Mouse Planet, All Ears.net, MGMStudios.org, and a few others.

Len went on the Snow White ride with us and I pointed out a few details that he had never noticed before while we discussed some of the changes from the rehab the previous year. He was particularly interested to hear about how the unloading redesign now caused cascading backups that affect the climax of the ride where the witch is pushing the rock over the ledge.

After the normal three laps around Snow White, we went to Cosmic Ray's for a bite to eat. To be honest, it was kind of nice to hang out with people who understand what it is like to do the same ride or hear the same audio queues over and over again.

My favorite story that I heard from them: that year they had added two psychologists to the staff in order to add some information to the guide about how to avoid meltdowns. To be able to do that, they needed to witness several typical family meltdowns in the park, so the two psychologists had the simple job of hanging around Main Street and watching for families that looked like ticking bombs. Then they would shadow them around the park, watching the progression throughout the day. These would then lead to the inevitable blow-up. What a job.

Eventually Len and the crew left to get to a media event at the Swan and Dolphin resort, and Ben went back for three more laps on SWSA. Since Ben was being so agreeable, we decided to try something new. We went to Epcot and took him on Soarin', which is a gentle hang gliding simulator. He had never been on it before, and it seemed like something he might possibly enjoy if we could just get him through the line.

He was more than happy to take the monorail over to Epcot and was even happy walking with us toward the Land pavilion where the Soarin' attraction is. Once we were inside the crowded pavilion, he was a little anxious but it was not too much. He did not complain when we got on the ride and he mostly seemed confused and a little bit scared.

The way Soarin' works is, when coming into the ride building there are three banks of seats that hang from a suspended structure. Each bank has three rows, and all of the seats are initially at ground level. Once everyone is seated and secured with belts, the banks rotate upwards so that the riders are now positioned completely off the ground and facing a giant movie screen. The size of the screen, combined with some gentle swaying in the seats, gives the rider the illusion of flying over a series of scenic locations in California, culminating in a nighttime flight over Disneyland just as the fireworks display is happening. Once the ride is over, the banks of seats rotate back down to floor level.

As it turned out, during our visit, the ride malfunctioned so that the seats never lifted up into position. We spent the full five minute ride cycle on the ground with the movie playing above us, which turned out to be a good thing because Ben heard the entire audio track and saw most of the film without any additional stress. After the movie finished the cast members working the attraction apologized for the problem and reset the ride. The second time through the seats swung up like they were supposed to, and Ben got to experience flying over California.

He never closed his eyes or covered his ears, and he never complained. I wouldn't say he loved the ride, but he surely didn't hate it. He mostly seemed to be just sort of taking it in and wasn't sure what to think. To me, it was a huge victory to see Ben enjoy a new ride in a different park for once.

As good as that particular day was, our frustrations with Ben's middle school only continued to grow. In grade school his teachers had sent home a notebook every day telling us what was going on with Ben in the classroom. At the middle school we found it very difficult to get any kind of timely information from his teacher. We had no concrete idea what Ben was actually doing in the classroom, and we became increasingly dissatisfied with that school in general and the teacher in particular. It came to a head one day in January of 2006 when Ben arrived home on the school bus sobbing inconsolably, missing all of his CDs, and wearing some other student's jacket.

We spent the next five days trying to get any kind of additional information from the teachers and classroom assistants regarding what had happened that day, with absolutely no response to our emails or telephone calls. Working up the food chain, we managed to meet with the vice principal of the school, who, in all fairness, seemed extremely and genuinely concerned, but the end result of that meeting was nothing more than concluding that we needed another meeting with more people. The combination of that meeting plus our impressions of seeing the activity in Ben's classroom that morning, led us to the conclusion that we could not, in good conscience, leave Ben at that school.

The most generous thing I can say on the topic is that it was not a classroom setting that we felt was appropriate to meet Ben's needs. I have quite a few less generous things to say about our experience with that school as well. I have elected not to recount them because doing so six years later would serve no useful purpose. We walked off of that campus, and Ben never set foot in that place again.

Fortunately, we had another option available to us in the form of Princeton House Charter School (PHCS). It is a school specifically designed for autistic children. Every single person on campus understands autism and knows how to interact with kids like Ben. Although the school had been recommended to us previously, it had not been a feasible option. They do not provide bus transportation, and we had no logistical way to get Ben to and from school every day. Since the time we had initially looked at that option, however, Sara had moved to a new home closer to PHCS. Kris and I had also purchased a house that was a reasonable drive away from the school.

The very same day that we removed Ben from the public middle school, we went up to the PHCS campus for a tour and were extremely impressed. The campus was very secure, gated all around such that it was impossible for a child to leave the property without an adult escort. The classrooms had a very low teacher to student ratio, and every teacher, therapist, and administrator we met seemed fantastic. Best of all, there was an open slot available due to another student who had recently moved out of state. We had a bit of paperwork to do, but within a matter of days Ben started at his new school and most of the behavior issues that we had seen in the past few months simply melted away.

As impressed as we were with the tour of the school, we were blown away by our first direct experience with Ben's new teacher. The first day that Sara dropped him off for class, the teacher noticed that Ben was still wearing diapers. When the teacher inquired as to why Ben was still wearing diapers at age twelve, Sara tried to explain to him how hard we had tried to potty train Ben but to no avail.

"No," the teacher said patiently, "we're done with that now. Send Ben to school tomorrow in regular underpants, and send in several changes of clothes. It's time for him to leave those pull-ups behind."

Needless to say, Sara and I were both skeptical but we did as Ben's teacher instructed. We figured we were in for months of battles, and endless loads of laundry. Instead, within two weeks Ben was consistently staying clean and dry all day long and was successfully using the bathroom with minimal prompting. Twelve years of wearing diapers had abruptly come to an end. We absolutely knew that Ben was in the right place.

Although Ben's overall behavior improved dramatically with the switch to Princeton House, his health seemed to be declining. His appetite had dropped to the point where he was just skin and bones. He seemed to catch every stray flu or cold that passed by. He got sick at school in the beginning of March, barely two months after starting at PHCS. He threw up several times before I could pick him up and take him to the doctor. His pediatrician told us that Ben had picked up a flu that was going around. Ben was sick as a dog for a full week. Then, at the beginning of April, he was sick again with the same kind of symptoms and it lasted for four days. Two weeks after that Ben vomited while on a field trip with his class.

We took him back to the doctor, who told us that as far as he could tell Ben was just fine. He had no signs of irritation in the ear/nose/throat department. His digestive system sounded good, and nowhere was anything inflamed. The likeliest cause for his most recent bout of vomiting was that during the long sickness the previous month he developed an irritation in the GI tract that had not yet fully healed and was therefore sensitive. If that were true, then it wouldn't take much to trigger vomiting. We left the office with a prescription for some meds to treat acid reflux and with the hope that they would keep Ben's stomach calm and allow it time to heal itself.

Herein lies one of the most difficult problems with kids like Ben who are essentially non-verbal: Ben had no way to describe what he was feeling. The doctors who examined Ben could only work from our outward description of his visible symptoms, plus whatever additional details they could glean from their own physical examination. If, for example, Ben had simply been able to say, "I have a sharp piercing pain in my gut right *here*" it would have saved him at least six months of agony. Instead, on the sixth of July in 2006 Ben wound up in the hospital for what would turn out to be the single most terrifying and emotionally draining experience of our lives.

Chapter 13

Five Weeks in Hell

By the beginning of July Ben's health had deteriorated so much that he was truly terrifying to look at. He ate so little that we were having active discussions with the doctors about the strong possibility of a feeding tube in order for him to get some nutrition. He slept almost non-stop and would often wake up long enough to vomit and then roll over to go back to sleep. The pediatrician had referred us to a GI doctor, and we were scheduled to see him later that week, but by the evening of July sixth he was in such a serious condition that we took him to the emergency room instead. He was given an initial ultrasound, which was inconclusive, so he was scheduled for a CT scan to look at his pancreas.

It was a very long night. Sara sat right by Ben's side the entire time while I hovered nearby. The IV in his arm drove him absolutely insane. He continually tried to pull it out, so either Sara or I had to remain awake and within arm's reach every single moment.

It was not until the middle of the night that he got the scan, and it took until the following morning before we finally got the results. In the meantime the doctor kept saying terrifying things like "serious liver damage" and "reduced blood clotting factor." We were all scared witless.

Finally after more than 36 hours in the emergency room, we received the official diagnosis of acute pancreatitis – an inflammation of the pancreas that causes severe pain, nausea, and a host of other symptoms. Left unchecked pancreatitis can lead to severe complications, up to and including death. Ben was admitted to the hospital and prescribed intravenous fluids with no food or drink by mouth. The prognosis was that within a week the pancreas should calm down.

Ironically, although extreme lethargy was one of the symptoms that had driven us to the emergency room in the first place, once Ben was admitted to the hospital it seemed like he barely slept. Rationally I know that was largely due to the fact that he was receiving IV fluids and nutrients and as a result he was not dehydrated or malnourished for the first time in possibly months. On top of that he was receiving proper pain medication. So again, it was likely the first time in ages that he did not have horrible abdominal pain. Combining both of those with legitimate anxiety about being in a strange place, confinement to a bed, and displacement from all of his familiar things, the result was a very wide awake and active boy.

For his first night in his room, I stayed up with him all night while Sara got what rest she could. She was physically exhausted from being awake with him throughout his day and a half in the emergency room.

Despite a sedative at 9pm, Ben never slept a wink. The next night Sara stayed with him all night while I got a little rest. Ben continued to be wide awake almost all of the time.

An entry from my personal journal from the fifth day he was in the hospital:

> *Ben was up all night Friday, and then slept from about 8:30am to 11am Saturday morning. He stayed awake all day, and through Saturday night. He napped for less than one hour on Sunday morning (roughly 8-9am), and again napped for 45 minutes in the evening, from 7-7:45pm. He is still awake now. By my math, in the past 48 hours he has slept less than five hours. He is currently wide awake. He does not look like he is fighting to stay awake, he is neither manic nor sluggish, he is simply ... awake. He shows no indication of sleeping anytime soon. For the last two nights he was given a sedative that should have knocked him out. The first night it made him woozy for fifteen minutes. Tonight I did not notice it affecting him in any way at all. How can he not be well past the point of collapse?*

That was the same day Ben had his first PICC line installed. A PICC line, or peripherally inserted central catheter, is essentially a more durable IV that has to be installed via a short surgical procedure in which a small flexible tube is inserted into a peripheral vein in the upper arm and then pushed in until the tip of the catheter is all the way into the chest near the heart. The procedure, which lasts about 30 minutes, involves a full surgical team and complete sedation and was frankly terrifying to witness. Unfortunately, over the course of Ben's hospital stay, the procedure would be repeated three more times due to Ben's determination to rip that catheter out of his own arm.

Tests showed that his liver function was impaired and that his blood clotting factor was significantly out of whack. His pancreas remained seriously inflamed, and his amylase and lipase levels were both extremely elevated. Those last two enzymes were the bellwether that the doctors were watching to indicate when his pancreas was beginning to settle down and work normally. When Ben was first admitted, the doctors explained that it usually took about a week of IV fluids and nutrients for those levels to drop to normal. When that happened, Ben could go home. At five days in, those numbers had not budged an iota.

On the sixth day I was lying on the bed next to Ben when he suddenly reached over and pulled the baseball cap off of my head. He ruffled my hair, put the cap back on me, then changed his mind and put it on his own head. It was a rare and welcome moment of levity after so many days of grim waiting.

The days wore on, and the news alternated between slight improvements which were followed by setbacks. About eleven days into his hospital stay the doctors decided to allow some solid food to see how he would handle it, and the result was his pancreatic enzymes shooting back up overnight.

Cap

Ben's mother and I were both nearly zombies by that point, living out each day in that hospital room in a kind of daze. Family came and went to offer their support and would frequently stay long enough for Sara or me to maybe run to our respective homes and take a shower or a nap. The doctors and nurses came in and out of the room at regular intervals, either to take blood for tests or deliver news about the results of those tests. Sara, being a teacher, was not yet missing any work since the school year had not started, but in another week she was due back in the classroom and would have to start burning through her very limited available sick time. I did my best to work from the hospital room on my laptop computer using the hospital's Wi-Fi signal when I could and used up my own vacation time when I couldn't. We had no moments of high drama; it was just one long, soul-crushing wait as we watched our son wasting away in a hospital bed.

More than two weeks into Ben's hospitalization, the primary doctor was still unsure what was causing the pancreatitis. In most cases the pancreas would have resumed normal function by then, but that just wasn't happening. One possibility was an autoimmune deficiency, but steroid treatment had no effect whatsoever. Another possibility was a pancreatic cyst; another CT scan showed that was not the case. What the scan did show, however, was that one of the ducts in the pancreas was larger than it should be and also larger than it had been two weeks earlier. The next step to finding out why the pancreatic duct was enlarged would be to perform a test called an Endoscopic Retrograde Cholangio-Pancreatography, or an ERCP for short. This is a procedure that combines endoscopy (looking inside the body with a camera mounted on a flexible tube) and fluoroscopy (using X-rays to capture real-time images). The problem was that nobody in Orlando was equipped to perform that test on a child. Because of the prevalence of non-invasive procedures like the ultrasound, an ERCP is rarely performed unless the doctor expects to do something like remove a stone or insert a stent. Because pancreatic stones are very rare among minors, the only doctors in the state with the skills and equipment to perform this procedure on a patient Ben's age were located almost 120 miles away at Shands Hospital in Gainesville, Florida. Shands is a teaching and research hospital, and employs many of the top medical professionals in the state of Florida.

It was late in the day on a Friday before the doctors finally reached the conclusion that an ERCP was indeed the necessary next step, but by then it was too late to start the process of arranging a transfer to Shands before the weekend. Because a transfer could only be arranged during normal Monday to Friday business office hours, Ben would have to suffer for another few days until the hospital could arrange for the transfer on Monday.

That particular Monday was July 24th, my first wedding anniversary with Kris and three years to the day since my family had moved to Florida. I had barely seen Kris in the previous few weeks, with all of my waking hours being spent at the hospital. We had long ago made reservations for dinner at the nicest and most romantic restaurant in the area, Victoria & Albert's at the Grand Floridian Resort in Walt Disney World. For a few hours that night I had some respite from the grinding terror of Ben's situation.

While Kris and I were celebrating our anniversary, Sara was riding with Ben in an ambulance for the nearly three hour drive to transport Ben to the hospital up in Gainesville. It was a harrowing experience for her, and Ben was plainly terrified the entire time. They had only just been placed into a room when I called to check on how the transfer went. I had not intended to drive up until the following morning, but Sara was so distraught by the experience of that ride that I immediately got into my car and drove there that night.

Our experience at Shands was like night and day compared to the nearly three weeks we had spent at the previous hospital. Where the last few weeks had consisted almost entirely of just sitting around and waiting, right from the start Ben's stay at Shands was a flurry of focused activity on the part of the hospital staff. Of course, no one winds up at Shands unless they have already exhausted all of the normal and mundane procedures. As a result, by the time a patient ends up there the doctors are by definition dealing with something both more complicated and more urgent.

Our very first morning there, the medical staff was buzzing around Ben with a focused intensity. To a person, every single nurse and doctor we met was uniformly excellent. The ERCP team came in to do a consult and evaluate Ben, and the GI doctor on that team was spectacular.

In addition, at some point Sara had mentioned to one of the nurses about how much Ben missed watching his video tapes and wondered if that might help him pass the time more easily. Astoundingly, the nurse called in a maintenance guy who proceeded to happily install a VCR in Ben's room. When Sara's mother came up for a visit later that day, she brought with her a large plastic bin containing literally dozens of Ben's tapes. Even in the midst of his pain and the confusion of his surroundings, he was clearly overjoyed.

Tuesday and Wednesday were spent having consultations with the various specialists as well as performing a variety of tests and blood work. It was the morning of Thursday, July 27th that Ben finally had the ERCP. We sat anxiously in Ben's empty hospital room waiting for word, and finally after about two hours we received the call from the nurse that Ben was coming out of surgery and we should head down to the recovery room to meet with the doctor. In a heartbeat we were down there, and shortly the doctor came in to talk to us. He said he had found "lots and lots" of stones blocking Ben's pancreatic duct. All of the stones had been removed, the duct widened, and a stent put in place to keep it open. He assured us that Ben had done very well during the surgery, and that he now had excellent flow through his entire pancreatic system. He told us that Ben should have complete relief from the pain immediately, although he couldn't say how much longer Ben would need to stay in the hospital.

Our relief was palpable, and we thanked the doctor profusely for finally getting to the root of the immediate problem. There was still the question to be resolved of how Ben had gotten the stones in the first place, and whether it would be a recurring problem. Finally, after more than three weeks and two hospitals, the crisis seemed to be resolved. We wished that it hadn't taken so long to reach that point, and we wished even more that Ben had not been in such pain for so many months. Everyone was ecstatic that Ben finally had some relief.

Once Ben recovered from the surgery and returned to his room, the change in his general demeanor was readily apparent. He was still terrifyingly thin and pale, but for the first time in months his normal happy personality began to shine through. Within two days he seemed like a brand new man. Unfortunately, after three days he began to run a fever and was showing signs of renewed pain.

By July 31st the doctors were concerned about a possible complication from the procedure, so they ordered another CT scan. By then we were approaching a month in the hospital, and all of the raw emotions were causing tempers to fray. Without question, every single family member wanted nothing more than for Ben to be healthy and happy, but we had all been stretched well beyond our breaking points.

Sara's mother had rented a townhouse at a nearby extended stay hotel where Sara would go rest and get cleaned up every day or two. They were kind enough to let me sleep there at least once, but I also made the hour and a half drive back to my own home more times than I can remember. Kris and my mom came to visit Ben a few times, and Sara's family was also a regular fixture at the hospital with her mother there almost constantly and her father and sister coming up to visit as often as possible. We were all exhausted and desperately worried about Ben.

More days passed, and the tests showed that Ben had developed a pseudo-cyst, or collection of fluid, at the top of his pancreas that had not been there prior to the ERCP. Such a growth is one of the potential side-effects that they had warned us about prior to the procedure. The doctor assured us that this was not a cause for alarm. Ben was started on a new antibiotic and was given acetaminophen for the fever and morphine for the pain. Hopefully the cyst would begin to resolve itself; otherwise the doctors might need to surgically drain the fluid. Once again we were left to watch and wait.

Another day went by, and Ben seemed to be in less pain. His fever began to go down as well, and it really and truly seemed like maybe this long nightmare was finally coming to a close. The doctor informed us that at that point he was only waiting for Ben's fever to completely resolve and for Ben to have a normal bowel movement before he could be released to go home. His amylase and lipase were both completely normal. His calcium level was perfect, his electrolytes were good, and by all indications Ben should be ready to leave the hospital very soon.

Still, day after anxious day went by and Ben continued to experience abdominal pain. His fever would go away, only to return the next day. August 1st turned into the second, third, fourth... The days rolled on and Benjamin hovered on the edge of being well enough to be discharged. On the seventh of August they did yet another CT scan and discovered two things: 1) good news that the pancreatic cysts were resolving nicely, and 2) bad news that Ben's large intestine was completely filled and distended with liquid.

Since the ERCP ten days prior, Ben had been experiencing the normal and expected pain following such a prolonged abdominal endoscopic procedure. For this pain he was given morphine, which has a common side effect of causing the muscles in the bowels to slow down or stop, resulting in constipation. Ben's bowels had been filling with fluid, but were not moving regularly enough to void the fluid. And so the not-so-virtuous cycle began: bloated and distended bowels cause cramps; Ben has cramps; Ben shows he is in pain; Ben gets more morphine; and morphine causes increased constipation. Lather, rinse, repeat.

All that needed to happen was for Ben to pass the fluid and the pain would go away. Sara started walking Ben all around the hospital in an effort to get things moving. Walk, walk, walk, sit on the commode and wait for something to happen, walk, walk, and walk some more. Finally, on the eighth of August and with the assistance of a suppository, Ben finally had a bowel movement of epic proportions. I don't want to dwell on the scatological, so suffice to say it was simply astonishing how much volume such a tiny kid produced. Immediately afterward? Ben had a look of pure bliss on his face, like the weight of the world had finally been lifted from his shoulders (or from his abdomen, as the case may be).

On August the eighth, nearly five full weeks after he had initially been admitted to the hospital, Ben finally went home. Where an average twelve year old of Ben's height weighs around 90 – 100 pounds, Ben weighed a mere 57 pounds the day he left the hospital. At least he was finally beginning to get some color back, though.

He spent another few days at home with the PICC line still in place so that he could finish a course of IV antibiotics, but before long he finally managed to pull that one out as well. He was rushed to the emergency room for x-rays to ensure that the entire tube had come out intact and that there were not any stray pieces of plastic floating loose in his bloodstream. Fortunately all was well, and he returned home with his mother and with a new IV line in place to continue the antibiotics at home. By the time he managed to pull that out a few days later, the doctors felt that he had received enough of the antibiotics to make it not worth going back and inserting yet another IV.

He was obviously feeling substantially better, so on Wednesday, August 16th he started the new school year nine days late. Life for him and me and everyone involved began to resume some kind of normalcy.

Chapter 14

Recovery, Relapse, Rides

Although it had been nearly a year and a half since SW1K, because of Ben's long illness his total ride count on Snow White's Scary Adventures was only up to 1,253. He had not fallen out of love with the ride, not by any means; he just had not felt up to visiting the Magic Kingdom much. On the first weekend after his return to school, he specifically asked to "take a tram", which is Ben-speak for asking to go to the Magic Kingdom. He was very happy indeed to be there for the first time in over two months. Even so, we went on SWSA only twice before running out of steam. As a matter of fact, it seemed like what he really wanted to do that entire weekend was to visit a whole bunch of places just to check and be sure they still existed.

I don't think he ever actually understood what the hospital was or had any notion that it was temporary. I really wonder if he just thought, "Okay, this is where I live now." Coupled with being in pain for so long, it must have been a terribly confusing experience for him. Now he was pain-free, probably for the first time in close to a year, and his energy was quickly returning.

A month after being released from Shands hospital he went back again for another ERCP in order to remove the stent from the previous surgery. It was a quick procedure, and within fifteen minutes of waking up afterwards he was dressed and ready to go home. He walked out of the hospital that day with a smile on his face and a bounce in his step.

The two big things we discovered during that follow-up were that his pancreatic enzyme function was seriously impaired, which means he must take an enzyme replacement supplement with every meal for the rest of his life, and that the root cause of all of his digestive troubles is Atypical Cystic Fibrosis. Essentially he has a mutation of the cystic fibrosis gene but does not have true cystic fibrosis. Apparently that requires two copies of the mutation whereas Ben has only one, which is known to cause episodes of pancreatitis. Needless to say, we watch him very closely now for any signs of abdominal distress.

Two months after leaving the hospital, Sara went to pick Ben up from school and received some astounding news: Ben's class had gone on a Community Inclusion field trip for lunch at McDonald's where his teacher got him the chicken nugget meal. She then told him that he had to eat the chicken before he got any fries, which he did without any complaining. What his teacher did not realize at the time was that that was the first time in *years* that Ben had eaten meat. Sara called me right away to tell me the news, and we were both ecstatic. On the way home from school she went through the McDonald's drive-thru and Ben ate a couple more chicken nuggets.

That day in October of 2006 was the pivotal turning point in Ben's overall health. It had taken a solid eight weeks to recover from the hospital experience, but he was finally starting to have a real appetite again. The specter of needing a feeding tube surgically installed was banished forever.

That winter Benjamin also became world famous, at least in a very tiny way. When the 2007 edition of the Unofficial Guide to Walt Disney World came out, the section for Snow White's Scary Adventures had a new paragraph added from the previous edition:

> *In 2005 we had the good fortune to experience Snow White with Ben, an autistic tyke who, with his family, has seen the attraction more than eleven hundred times. His parents — far better people than us — stay sane by thinking of ways to redesign the attraction each time through.*

That paragraph would remain in every new edition of the Guide through 2012. Sadly, the 2013 edition no longer has any entry at all for Snow White's Scary Adventures.

By the spring of 2007 Ben was eating a variety of new foods and was steadily gaining weight. He was still smaller than he should have been for his age, but he was catching up nicely and seemed so much more energetic than he had been only a few months before. He was back to visiting the Disney parks with some regularity, and while his ride count on Snow White continued to inch up he also expanded his interests to other areas of the parks. Then one Sunday in late March he gave us a new scare.

He had not eaten since the day before, was not even drinking any juice, and he was more-or-less living in the bathroom. After everything we had gone through the previous summer, all of the red flags went up. When he showed no improvement by the next morning, Sara took off Monday from work to stay home with him and call doctors. When she described the symptoms to the GI specialist, the doctor doubted that the symptoms had anything to do with pancreatitis. Late that afternoon Ben saw the pediatrician, who also did not think the symptoms looked like pancreatitis. Even so, Ben was clearly dehydrated by that point and the pediatrician suggested that we take him to the emergency room at the local children's hospital to get some blood work and an IV.

By then I was able to join Sara and Ben, and we sat through a very long night in the ER. It was well after midnight before a doctor was able to see Ben. Blood work was done, a stool sample was taken, and Ben was rehydrated with a saline solution in the IV drip. He started perking up about halfway through the IV, and even started drinking juice without prompting. All of the tests came back basically OK except for the dehydration and an elevated white blood count. Around 4am Ben was released from the hospital, and he and his mother returned home to rest.

Later that day Sara called to say that Ben was still barely eating, he wasn't drinking at all, and was becoming increasingly lethargic. Clearly something was still going on, something that the ER doctor had missed. Sara had calls out to the pediatrician and GI doc and was justifiably not taking "it's just the flu" as an answer. She was not about to let Ben start another six-month round of suffering, and I wholeheartedly agreed. It was the following morning before Ben was able to see the nurse at the GI doctor's office for another exam.

At that visit they did something new that had not been done in the emergency room the previous day, namely an abdominal x-ray. It showed that Ben's bowels were fully impacted, filled to capacity. Ben was not eating or drinking because there was simply nowhere for the food to go. The doctor prescribed some laxatives and suppositories to help clear the blockage and sent Sara and Ben home.

What followed was another 24 hours of pure agony for Ben. He had still not passed anything, and the new medications were causing severe abdominal cramps. I went over to Sara's place to try to help, and Ben was literally *screaming* in pain every few minutes as he would get the cramps. Sara got on the phone with the doctor and was practically in tears begging him to please help. He instructed us to bring Ben back to the hospital, and the doctor would meet us there to perform a manual disimpaction in which Ben would be placed under sedation and then the doctor would manually clear Ben's bowels as far as possible.

We quickly arrived at the hospital, and then waited anxiously as Ben was taken back for the procedure. We sat in the waiting room, wondering if this was what life was going to be like now with every few months spent in hospitals and Ben's life devolving into a never-ending cycle of pain. It was so unfair to have seen him so happy and healthy for the past few months and then to wind up right back where we started.

After 45 minutes of waiting, the doctor came out to give us the startling news. As it turns out, Ben had been completely blocked up by paper. Yes, paper. The doctor shook his head and said that he had done literally thousands of manual disimpactions in his career, and out of all of those procedures Ben's was the first one that did not stink to high heaven because almost everything that came out was paper.

We had noticed that Ben had started eating things like the wrappers from crayons, toilet tissue from the roll, and things like that. Apparently it all created a natural plug that would not allow anything else to move.

After about two hours in the recovery room, we returned to Sara's home so that Ben could rest. Although he was exhausted he must have been feeling better because on the way there he asked to stop at McDonald's for some chicken and fries. It was the first time in six days that he had asked for food.

One thing that Sara pointed out, as Ben settled into his nice comfy bed for a nap, was that this was the first time in all of his thirteen years that his autism had landed him in the hospital. He had fractured his arm once while roller skating, but that was a normal kid thing. The previous year's bout with pancreatitis would have happened regardless of his autism. This eating paper thing, though, was a classic autistic behavior. Clearly we, along with the assistance of his teachers, had our work set out for us in order to deal with it. At least pica, the medical term for a desire to eat non-nutritious materials like paper, dirt, or hair, was a known behavioral issue with established successful strategies for combating it.

Throughout 2007 Ben continued to grow bigger and stronger, and at Disney he became much more willing to spend more time on other rides. By June he willingly went on a water ride, the Jungle Cruise, and he even enjoyed it.

In August he went to one of the Disney water parks for the first time ever. Although he complained every step of the way from the drive to parking to getting through the turnstiles, as soon as he got inside and saw the wave pool he was in heaven. He wasn't content just to stand in the shallow end and let the waves splash around him. No, he aggressively swam to the deepest part of the wave pool where the water was well over his head and he threw himself into the oncoming waves with wild abandon. When he tired of that after a full hour, he tried some of the water slides and loved them just as much. All total he spent more than three hours soaking up the sun, and the next morning he begged to go back from the moment he woke up. It was absolutely glorious to see him so healthy and energetic, having the time of his life. It was such a complete transformation from the weak and sickly child he had been just one year before.

By October he was up to 1,688 rides on Snow White's Scary Adventure, and one night we took him to Mickey's Not-So-Scary Halloween Party. This is a special event on select autumn nights in the Magic Kingdom where Disney dresses up the park with special Halloween decorations and lighting and has trick-or-treating for all of the guests. Since Ben did not usually visit the park after dark, he had fun enjoying the novelty of seeing all of the spooky lighting and such. And of course, he absolutely *loved* all the candy.

At one point late in the evening, as we were just finishing another lap around SWSA, we saw Snow White herself walk by with all seven dwarfs marching in a row behind her. Benjamin practically jumped out of his skin at that sight. We took him over to meet her, and came away with these two awesome photos (shown below one above the other):

Halloween

He was so delighted it was infectious.

One of the advantages of the Halloween party is that it is much less crowded than a normal day in the park since it is a special-ticket event with a hard cap on the number of tickets that can be sold. Because of the lessened crowd that night, on top of the dozen times he went on Snow White's Scary Adventures, he also saw Pirates of the Caribbean, Haunted Mansion, Small World, Winnie the Pooh, the Tomorrowland Transit Authority, and Buzz Lightyear. It was an awesome night all around.

Ben was fully back up to speed, he was doing well in school, and his time spent in the Disney parks was still showing great progress in his social and life skills. Soon enough 2007 turned into 2008, and by March he was rapidly approaching 2,000 rides on Snow White's Scary Adventures. As we started to prepare for SW2K, it turns out that Disney was doing some special planning of their own.

Chapter 15

SW2K

As Ben's ride count grew ever closer to the next big milestone, I sought the assistance of an acquaintance of mine, Carl Bond, an area manager at Epcot in the entertainment division. Aware of my son's passion for Snow White, Carl reached out to Scott Cook, Carl's counterpart at the Magic Kingdom.

At the time Disney had a special "Year of a Million Dreams" program, which, ironically, ran for just over two years. As a part of the program, select cast members were assigned to the Dream Squad and instructed to go out and make dreams come true. During that period, in any of the Disney theme parks, members of the Dream Squad walked around wearing special white vests over their regular uniform and randomly did unexpected things such as handing out a Dream Fastpass to a family so that small group could use the alternate Fastpass entrance at every ride in the park for the whole day. One of the lead Dream Squad members in the Magic Kingdom was David Storm, an amazing man that had been given the task by Scott Cook to create a dream-come-true experience for Benjamin.

The big day arrived on Saturday, March 8th. Ben had reached 1,990 rides the previous Wednesday, so the entire family was very excited for that weekend.

We had coordinated in advance with David regarding when we would arrive in the park and approximately when we expected the 2,000th ride to happen. We were instructed to check in with City Hall as soon as we were inside the park. Ben would go to the park with Kris and me, and then Sara and her parents would meet us there for all the hoopla.

The three of us arrived at the Magic Kingdom parking lot at around noon and made our way to the Ticket and Transportation Center in order to catch the monorail to the park. Before we boarded the monorail, we stopped at one of the ticket windows in order to reprint a lost ticket, and when the cast member heard about Ben's big milestone that day she gave him an "Honorary Citizen" pin to celebrate. Ben wore that button proudly all day. With our tickets in order we proceeded to the monorail, and then around to the Magic Kingdom itself.

Ben was buzzing with excitement, although I don't think he realized this day would be any different than any of our hundreds of previous visits to the park. As usual, he had his headphones on and was listening to Disney music on his iPod. And thank goodness for the iPod! It was such a huge improvement over lugging a CD player and discs everywhere.

We went through the turnstiles, passed under the train station, and then walked straight to City Hall as previously instructed. Once there, a cast member phoned David and spoke to him briefly before informing us where we should go on Main Street to meet him. We left City Hall, crossed the street to enter the Main Street Confectionary, and then proceeded on through to the gift shop next door. Ben was admiring some lighted shadowbox scenes on one of the glass shelves when David appeared through an Employee-Only door.

David was a towering man, well over six feet tall, and Ben took an immediate liking to David's infectious smile. As he met Benjamin for the first time, David seemed genuinely excited about Ben's whole Snow White experience. He informed us that they were holding a special seat of honor for Ben and the family in order to view the afternoon parade, and that he had something spectacular planned afterwards for the actual 2,000th ride. He stressed that if there was anything he could do to make the day more comfortable for Ben to please let him know, and with that he disappeared again backstage, through the Employee-Only door with a final farewell.

Once David departed Ben made a bee line to the Snow White ride for his first three rides of the day, bringing his total to 1,993. Kris and I followed along right behind as Ben practically skipped his way through the park. Following his first set on Snow White he bounced over to The Many Adventures of Winnie the Pooh for a quick ride. As he exited from there he looked up at me and said, "Daddy. I want. Some fries. Please."

Spaced almost directly between Pooh and Snow White is the Village Fry Shoppe. I sometimes wonder if Disney installed it specifically for Ben. Our happy trio meandered back over to the quick service counter, and in short order Ben had a tray with a nice fresh order of fries on it.

At this point I have to note that, much in the spirit of Pooh, it was a very blustery day. It wasn't particularly cold or rainy, but the wind was gusting enough to be very noticeable. We found a vacant table in the Fantasyland courtyard and Ben sat down with his tray full of fries ready for devouring. But before he could even take his first bite, a gust of wind came along and sent the whole thing flying. The poor people at the next table found themselves on the receiving end of a shower of fries, and Ben let out a desperate wail. It was like it was happening in slow motion, with Ben screaming, "Nooooooooooooooo!" as his fries sailed away.

I quickly cleaned up the mess, and then as Kris sat with Ben to console him I went back to the Fry Shoppe to replace Ben's lost afternoon snack. Amazingly, when I mentioned what had happened, the cast member at the fry shop was kind enough to replace the fries free of charge. We then found a more sheltered spot for Ben to sit and enjoy his meal, take two. He was very much relieved and wolfed down his food in a matter of minutes before getting a sly look on his face and declaring, "Daddy. I want. More Snow White. Please!"

After another set of rides on Snow White, bringing his total to 1,996, Ben led us first into Sir Mickey's gift shop and then just out the door to his favorite bench. He sat there happily for several minutes, kind of people watching, until he suddenly looked up at me again and tilted his head. "Daddy. I want. Pirates. Please!"

Over the past few months he had finally gotten over his phobia of water rides and had newly discovered the coolness of Pirates of the Caribbean. With great dexterity he wove his way through the Fantasyland crowds, with Kris and me in tow, as he strode down the curved walkway past the castle and into Liberty Square. With a turn to the left he threaded between the Liberty Bell and the Stockades, and then we were into Frontierland. As usual, his route took us past the Country Bear Jamboree and into the bakery next door before crossing into another gift shop. I'm not sure whether he avoids the streets because of the crowds, because of the air conditioning in the shops, or for some other reason known only to him. In any case, he made a quick zag out of the gift shop and into the Pecos Bill Tall Tale Inn and Café next door where he wended his way all the way through the seating area and out the exit that borders

Adventureland. With that we were at the entrance to Pirates and proceeded to have a grand old time floating through the adventures of Captain Jack Sparrow.

The return route from Pirates followed the same path since for some reason Ben actively avoids walking through Adventureland. But we had a minor crisis: the candy store was apparently all out of his then-favorite candy, Nerds. After three successive shops it became apparent that the Magic Kingdom was experiencing some kind of global shortage, and Ben was on the verge of tears. In the third shop, which was next to Mickey's PhilharMagic in Fantasyland, I tactfully suggested to him that maybe he should get Sprees instead. He grudgingly agreed and a complete meltdown was averted. With that resolved, he took three more trips on Snow White, and he was up to 1,999 rides.

The timing was perfect. We left Fantasyland and walked back down Main Street just ahead of the 3:00 parade which was approaching from the Adventureland side of the park. We made it to City Hall just before the parade reached that point, and there in front was Sara and her parents as well as a Dream Squad member holding a private bench for us. Ben ran to his mom to give her a big hug and had big smiles for Grandma and Grandpa as well. He sat on the bench perched happily between his mom and his grandpa, and for the first time in his life he actually sat and watched the entire Disney parade. One of the very last floats featured Snow White and Prince Charming surrounded by the Seven Dwarfs, with the Wicked Queen glowering at them from her own platform. Ben watched that particular float very intently.

Once the parade was over, our entire group went into City Hall and we let them know we were there for David's surprise. I expected David to come out to greet us; I did not expect to be greeted by an entire phalanx of Dream Squad cast members. Ben seemed flattered by all the attention. After socializing for a few minutes, yet another Dream Squad member came out to tell us they were ready. We were all escorted behind the counter and into the VIP room in the back.

I had been told in advance that Ben was getting a private meet and greet with Snow White. Beyond my expectations was to see Snow White, all seven dwarfs, Prince Charming, the Wicked Queen, plus a professional photographer and numerous other cast members. The entire group from the Snow White parade float was there in the room and focused entirely on Benjamin. He was completely gob-smacked.

He waded into the crowd of characters, bewildered at all of them, and greeted each of them in turn. In the background a photographer was busy snapping away while Ben tentatively reached out to touch the Wicked Queen and then shook the hand of Prince Charming. One perfect moment was when Snow White herself leaned down and kissed him on the cheek, leaving a big red lipstick mark. Ben got a little bashful, and then he took a step forward and had a huge grin on his face as he gave Snow White a big hug. That lipstick mark stayed on his face for the rest of the day, with Ben even refusing to wash it off at bedtime. He touched several of the dwarfs, posed for some group photos, and soaked it all in.

Kiss

Eventually Snow White apologized to Ben, saying it was time for her to take all of the dwarfs back to their cabin because it was their nap time. With one final round of hugs it was time for us to leave City Hall and walk back to Fantasyland for the 2,000th ride.

I expected David to walk us over, which he did, but he was also joined by an army of cast members flanking our group on both sides and clearing a path through the crowds. On his radio David called ahead to let the folks at the ride know that we were coming, and then again when we were about to walk around the corner. The cast members cut a path for us, and Ben was escorted directly into the loading area and onto a mine cart.

He sat in the front row with his mom, Kris and I sat behind them, and his grandparents sat in the back. A photographer stood to the side taking pictures of the whole thing as we rolled forward past the Wishing Well and onward through the doorway into darkness.

For me the ride itself was pretty much like it had been for the last 1,999 times, honestly there just weren't any surprises left in there, but Ben seemed to love it just as much as every other time he had been on it. When our mine cart emerged through the final door three minutes later, the photographer was waiting to snap more photos. I thought that was the big finale, but I quickly discovered I was completely mistaken.

As soon as we got off the ride, we saw that a huge crowd had formed and at the center was a giant sign commemorating Ben's 2,000th ride signed by Snow White and all seven dwarfs. Another cast member held a display with a beautiful custom framed picture of Snow White and the dwarfs, also autographed by all of them, plus some collector's pins, a Snow White cup, another picture frame, and a pile of jewels. The photographer continued to take pictures as David announced to the entire crowd what Ben had just achieved, and then everyone cheered. Ben came forward, and upon his head they placed a pair of Mickey Mouse Club mouse ears with his name embroidered on the back. He wore that iconic black hat for the rest of the day, not taking it off until he crawled into bed late that night. For a kid that never, ever wears hats, that was pretty exceptional. We were all completely overwhelmed by the whole thing and thanked David profusely for arranging such an exceptional event for Ben.

Of course, once all the hoopla was over, well, actually, *before* all the hoopla was over, Ben turned around to go back to the ride. This made perfect sense, in that he still had two more rides to go in that particular set. The rest of the family stayed behind to continue to thank all of the wonderful Disney cast members, and it was just Ben and me on that 2,001st ride. The whole time through he beamed a huge, contented smile. Now that he was in his quiet space, with just me and his favorite ride, he relaxed enough to show just how much he had enjoyed the whole thing.

We spent another hour or so in the park before Ben finally got tired and asked to leave. Altogether he went on the ride fourteen times that day and had a wonderful time hanging out with so many family members.

Not long after the big ride I received a phone call from the Disney photographer who wanted my mailing address so that he could send out a photo CD with all of the pictures from that day. Between the value of all of those pictures, the gifts they gave Ben, and the time and labor that was put into making the event happen, Disney invested hundreds, if not thousands, of dollars to make one autistic boy feel special for a day. That is not something that our family will soon forget.

Later that night, as I reflected on the day's experience, I pondered the fact that every time I walk into that park with Ben, not just on that day but on *every single visit*, I am struck by just how much Disney has done for my son. People like David Storm have had a direct, lasting, positive impact on his life. Virtually every cast member who works in Fantasyland has, at one time or another, stopped and done a little something for Ben to make his day more magical. It seemed as though Walt Disney himself, who passed away decades before Ben was born, had reached across time, all the way from 1937, in order to bring Ben a never-ending source of happiness.

I didn't know what was in store for Ben in the future. I worried about what would happen when he was an adult; what would happen when his mother and I are no longer here to take care of him. But for that weekend at least, I was content with our son's well being. I owe an important part of that to the Walt Disney Company and all that they have collectively done. For that I am eternally grateful.

Chapter 16

SW3K

Following the tremendous high of the SW2K celebration, things returned to normal. Ben visited the Magic Kingdom three or four times per month, he did well in school, and he continued to be healthy. By the fall of 2009 he looked nothing at all like the pale scarecrow of a kid who he had been during his long illness. He had more than doubled in weight and had a healthy glow about him.

A typical visit to the Magic Kingdom was no longer Snow White-centric. To be sure, he would go on that ride several times each time we were at the park, but it was no longer the first place he wanted to go and it did not dominate his time. Somewhere along the way, he discovered the Fantasia store located inside the Contemporary Hotel, so it was very common for him to want to take the monorail to the Contemporary where he would spend some time looking at the enchanted broom statues that lined the top shelves throughout the store. Then we would take the escalators down three flights to street level and walk from there to the Magic Kingdom entrance.

Once inside the park he might spend a lengthy amount time browsing through the shops on either side of Main Street or sitting outside the first aid station tucked away in a quiet niche between Casey's

Corner and the Crystal Palace where he would people watch. During a normal day at the park he would walk to nearly every section of the Magic Kingdom, although he never did like Mickey's Toontown Fair, which has since been replaced by the Storybook Circus. Sometimes he would only want to get on the big train and ride the Walt Disney World Railroad all the way around for two or three complete laps.

Even the time he spent at Snow White's Scary Adventures was subtly changing. He still almost always went in sets of three, but the time between each of those rides within the sets grew longer. He seemed to enjoy just hanging out in the alternate entrance and either looking at the mural or peering inside the end of the ride whenever the doors were open in order to catch a glimpse of the scene with Prince Charming kissing Snow White. Whereas in the early days each set of three rides would happen in rapid fire, done in ten minutes; now each might take a half hour or more because of all the time he spent just hanging out off to the side and out of other people's way.

He still carried his iPod everywhere, with his headphones on nearly the all the time; he had also taken an interest in photography. For a few years he carried around a big red Disney digital camera that was designed specifically for kids. When that camera eventually died, after a long and full life, he graduated to a Nikon Coolpix that went with him everywhere. He became very good at framing and taking photos and snapped several good shots of the loading area mural at Snow White's Scary Adventures.

One Saturday afternoon, on the second weekend in September of 2009, Ben and I were in the park for a normal visit. On the other side of the country Disney held the first D23 Expo in Anaheim, California, the home of Disneyland. D23 is the official Disney fan club, the D referring to Disney; the 23 referring to 1923, the year when Walt Disney arrived in Hollywood and founded the company. Prior to the D23 Expo, it was a very poorly kept secret that Disney would be announcing a major Fantasyland expansion at this event; the only mystery was the details of the expansion. All that afternoon as Ben and I stood in lines at various rides (mostly Snow White), I continually checked the web browser on my phone for updates from the Expo. Finally the official news broke, and it was excellent: a new Little Mermaid dark ride, a Beauty and the Beast themed restaurant, a big Disney Princess meet and greet, but most importantly Snow White's Scary Adventures was not being touched.

I was ecstatic because I figured that if Disney was going to spend that much money in Fantasyland without altering or removing Ben's ride, then it was almost certainly safe for at least a decade and probably more. Since the expansion would take three or four years to complete, it would be a long while before the company looked at spending more money and making more changes in that section of the park.

I happened to see the area manager walking by and flagged her down to tell her how excited I was by the news. At first she was a little cagey, in that "I can neither confirm nor deny" mode, until I showed her that Disney Parks Chairman Jay Rasulo had made the official announcement. At that point she gushed about how excited they all were about the new expansion. She had, of course, known about it for a while but was forbidden to say anything. We talked a bit more before Benjamin finally ran out of patience and pulled me back to his ride and I cheerily waved goodbye. Ben had a great time that day, walking around to all the sections of the park and spending surprisingly little time at the Snow White ride itself, although he finished the day with a new grand total of 2,865 rides.

With the 3,000th ride approaching, I tried to contact the people who had been involved with SW2K. Unfortunately David Storm, who had done such an amazing job organizing the last celebration, had recently left the company to go back to school. After several missed connections, it appeared that SW3K was going to be a bit anti-climactic. To be perfectly clear, although I was certainly a little disappointed, I was never in any way upset with Disney. They had done amazing things for my family. I certainly did not feel like they owed us anything.

The 3,000th ride happened on a bitterly cold day at the beginning of January, 2010. When I say bitterly cold, I am sure there are plenty of people in Wisconsin who would roll their eyes at me. But it really was genuinely cold, not just Florida-cold but actual hovering-around-the-freezing-point cold. For more than a week the temperatures had been in the 20s, and regardless of where you live, below freezing is, well, *freezing*.

When Ben and I arrived at the park that morning we had to stop at a gift shop and buy us each a new sweater and some gloves. The jackets we were wearing were not nearly warm enough. When Sara arrived shortly thereafter, she brought Ben yet another layer of warm clothes while she herself was bundled up in a heavy jacket, gloves, and a stocking cap. Kris and my mother also came for the 3,000th ride. Sara's parents were unfortunately unable to make it that day.

Disney made up a commemorative certificate to celebrate the 3,000th ride, presenting it to us in front of a small crowd as we exited the attraction. Ben had a good time despite the cold. In the end, it was a fun day in the park, and while not quite as dramatic or

exciting as SW1K or SW2K it was certainly a perfectly
fine (if somewhat chilly) day.

3,000 Rides

Not long after the three thousandth ride a rumble
began around the internet that the plans for the
Fantasyland expansion were being changed. The
rumors persisted throughout 2010, and by the end of
the year the noise coming from the Disney-sphere
was that the huge Princess meet and greet was going
to be replaced by kid-friendly roller coaster called The
Seven Dwarfs' Mine Ride. With the addition of a very
large Snow White themed attraction, the next logical
change was for Snow White's Scary Adventures to be
eliminated. I first heard that particular rumor in late
December. A knot formed in the pit of my stomach.

On January 18th, 2011, Disney made their official
announcement: the Seven Dwarfs Mine Ride was

going to be built, and Snow White's Scary Adventures would be closed and replaced with a smaller scale meet and greet called Princess Fairytale Hall. No closing date was announced for SWSA, but we knew that the end was near.

We had no way to explain it to Ben, no way that he would understand. We hoped that in the end it would be a positive thing, a final break from his obsession that would help him grow and move on. Still, it was heartbreaking news for all of us, and we worried what would happen.

Another year went by before the actual closing date was announced. The final day of operation would be Thursday, May 31st, 2012.

By the time that announcement was made in February, it had been more than two years since SW3K. Ben's total ride count was only up to 3,298 rides. He had reached a point where he only went there maybe once or twice per month, and I began to feel like the closing would be okay. By then I also had learned more about the coming new attractions, particularly the Journey of the Little Mermaid ride. I knew that Ben would really like the expansion. The new Little Mermaid ride was longer than SWSA and filled with all of the music that Ben loved. I wished that it would open before Snow White closed, but that just wasn't going to happen. All we could do was hope for the best, and try to make Ben's last day with

Snow White's Scary Adventures as memorable as possible.

Chapter 17

The Final Night

We didn't know how the end would go. The only certain thing was that we needed to be there for the last night of operation for Snow White's Scary Adventures, giving Ben the opportunity to say goodbye. We actually discussed it with his autism specialist, and she agreed that the best thing for him would be to make a kind of ceremony out of it to help him process the event. And so we made our plans for that night; I would get Ben from school and bring him to the park, Sara would meet us there as soon as she was done with work, and we would stay until the bitter end. Knowing how emotionally and physically draining it would be, we let his teachers know that he would not be in school the next day. I arranged my schedule to keep him home on the day after the closing so that he could decompress. For better or worse, it was the beginning of the end.

Ben and I arrived at the park at about 5pm that night. He was in a very good mood, excited about being at the Magic Kingdom on a weekday evening. He spent a small amount of time walking through the big gift shop on Main Street, cut through Casey's Corner across towards Adventureland, and then took the bridge over to Ye Olde Christmas Shoppe in Liberty Square. At the time, he had a bit of a crush on Tinkerbell, and the Christmas shop had an entire wall of Tink ornaments. After several minutes of looking, he finally decided on a new ornament. Once it was safely wrapped and boxed, he looked at me and said, "Daddy... I want... Snow White... please!"

In nine years of constant visits, I had never seen a line for SWSA like the one we encountered that night. Under normal circumstances the alternate entrance might occasionally back up to the swinging door by the ride exit. On this night at 5:30pm the line for the handicap entrance was out the door and all the way around to where the regular line starts. The main line was packed all the way out to the stroller parking area next to the attraction. It seemed like everyone was taking pictures and talking about wanting to get in one last ride before it went away forever.

We got in line and before long we were in the mine cart for Ben's 3,452nd ride on SWSA. Earlier in the year we had thought maybe Ben would reach 3,500 rides before it closed. I had long since concluded that just wasn't going to happen. I figured we would let Ben ride as many times as he wanted that night, and he would finish somewhere in the 3,460s or 3,470s.

One memorable incident occurred during the fourth ride of the evening. A woman who had transferred from a wheelchair was riding in the mine cart ahead of us. She had a great deal of trouble getting into the cart, and I knew that she would have some difficulty getting back out once the ride was over. As it turns out, when her cart reached the unloading zone at the end of the ride she was quite literally stuck. Ben and I were one stop back, sitting in the Happily Ever After scene. I could see exactly what was going on.

I felt so awful for that poor woman, as she was completely stuck and her companions were struggling to help get her free. After about a minute the ride went into Emergency Stop mode and the house lights came up. For several minutes the cast members assisted the stuck rider. I have no doubt that she felt like hundreds of eyes were staring at her and her struggles. I can only imagine her distress.

Meanwhile, as the minutes rolled on, I began to worry that Ben would get stressed out by the delay. As it turns out, I had nothing to fear because Ben had his camera with him. He loved taking photos and had tried to take pictures on his ride in the past, but they never turned out well. In particular, he had tried and tried to get a picture of the Prince waking Snow White with Love's First Kiss. Sitting there in the back row of the mine cart, I saw Ben's eyes light up when he realized that the lights were on, the cart wasn't moving, and he had his camera. He very carefully turned around and held out the camera, taking exquisite care to line up the perfect shot. He snapped two or three pictures and was extremely satisfied with the results on the camera's screen.

Shortly after that, the cart in front of us was finally cleared. As near as I can tell, the woman was uninjured and was able to carry on with her companions in enjoying the park. I truly hope that experience did not ruin her visit.

In any case, that was my first inkling that it was truly going to be an exceptional night. What should have been a crisis point that would tip Ben into a full-on meltdown instead became the happiest of accidents for him. Everything was breaking his way. He was smiling ear to ear with that infectious grin of his.

As we exited the mine cart from that ride, we saw that Sara had arrived. Benjamin greeted her with a smile, and then took her hand and led her back into line for the next ride. I left the two of them to catch up and have some Mama time while I went to get a couple bottles of red Powerade for Ben and a cold drink for myself.

As Ben and his mom continued doing laps on the ride, very slow laps since the line just wasn't letting up, I could see cast members gathering nearby. Stacey Patrone, the cast member who had taken ownership of creating a special moment for Ben, arrived on the scene and let us know that at 7pm she had a surprise for Ben if we didn't mind joining her at the appointed time. At 7:01pm Ben went on his 3,458th ride with his mother beside him and with me in the seat right behind. Three minutes later we exited the ride to find Stacey waiting for us with a big smile on her face, inviting us to come for a short walk with her. Ben was about to have his truly Magical Moment.

Earlier in the week, a few days before the final night of Snow White's Scary Adventures, I had had a telephone conversation with Stacey. We discussed the possibilities for creating a Magical Moment for Benjamin on the last evening and coordinated times and such. She couldn't give me any specifics, but we arranged that whatever happened would be at 7pm. I was very careful to stress to her that my family did not *expect* Disney to do anything for Ben yet we were extremely grateful for anything that they *did* do.

My one concern had to do with expectations. I was a little worried that whatever they did, Ben might not seem like he was enjoying it. Someone who doesn't know Ben can find it kind of hard to read him, and he can also get overwhelmed if too many people are focused on him. I warned her not to necessarily expect anything like a Kodak moment but reassured her that, whatever she put together, I was sure that Ben would enjoy in his own way.

So there we were on the closing night, just after 7pm, being led by Stacey and a couple other cast members to stand over in front of The Friar's Nook just around the corner. Ben was in a happy mood but wanted to pull us back over towards SWSA since he was having the time of his life and wanted to get right back to it. After a few short minutes of waiting, a door opened and out came Snow White herself to come talk to Ben. All of a sudden, a huge smile filled Ben's face and he started laughing hysterically. He was positively transfixed. That Kodak moment that I warned Stacey not to expect? Oh yeah, it was there in spades.

Ben Meets Snow White

Snow White continued to talk to him as Ben very shyly took her hand and then laughed some more. It was an almost drunken laugh, the laugh you hear from a baby when you play peek-a-boo for too long and they drift into that delirious-happy state. As Snow White talked to him about the ride, and about all of the dwarfs, Ben seemed to be absolutely glowing with joy. A crowd began to gather behind him. I had to take off my glasses to dry my eyes. I can assure you that I am the manliest of men and I am positive it was just allergies or perhaps a speck of dust that got in my eye. Whatever it was, it seemed to be spreading to everyone nearby. There was not a dry eye in the house.

This went on for several minutes and Snow White never let up, never broke character even for a moment. She knew how many times Ben had been on her ride, she knew what his favorite moments in the ride were, and most of all she knew how to keep him engaged and joyously happy. Eventually she invited Ben to go on the ride with her. He gleefully agreed. Stacey led the parade with Ben and Snow White, Sara, several other cast members (including two photographers), and myself. The crowd parted in front of us and we were guided straight to the front of the line. The entire time, Snow White kept up with her unending improvised monologue and Ben kept up with his boisterous laughter.

3333333

Soon we were in the mine cart. One of the photographers joined us to continue snapping pictures of the encounter. Snow White would point out details of the ride. Ben would alternately turn away from her and then spin back around and take her hand. The poor boy was fully twitterpated.

Exiting the Ride (photo courtesy of Kevin Yee)

The ride ended, but the visit wasn't over yet. Stacey led us through the exit gate as the crowd cheered for Ben. I didn't know it at the time, but Kevin Yee from MiceAge.com was there taking photos and he caught what turned out to be my favorite shot of the night. You can see Ben still electric with joy, holding Snow White's hand as the crowd looks on.

We were led back over to The Friar's Nook, and Snow White continued to visit with Ben for several more minutes. Stacey presented Ben with a CD full of photos from inside the ride, taken earlier that morning by one of the Disney photographers so that he would have some high quality pictures to remember the ride. Altogether Snow White spent about fifteen minutes with Ben. The entire time he was enchanted by her presence, even though he knew it couldn't last forever. Finally Snow White bid Ben farewell, apologizing that she could not leave Dopey alone in the cottage for very long and she had to get back to him. With one last kiss she whirled away and disappeared as Ben looked on.

After Snow White was gone, Ben immediately turned to his mom. "Mama... I want... more Snow White... PLEASE!"

Now, I haven't been on the ride quite as many times as Ben but I've probably been there for at least 3/4 of them. Most of them were pretty much the same. But I must say that ride number 3,459 was pretty exceptional. I thought to myself, wow — it just doesn't matter what else happened that night because it just couldn't get any better.

Farewell Sweet Princess

And then it got better.

Having just spent fifteen solid minutes with Snow White, we thought that Benjamin would need to take a few minutes to digest what had just happened, or even that he might try to follow her to the door she disappeared through. No, Ben just let out another laugh and then led us back for another round on Snow White's Scary Adventures. His mother and I were still reeling from how amazing the visit was; Ben was ready to keep going full steam ahead. As he took both our hands and pulled us back to his ride, the best we could do was turn back and mouth "thank you so much!" to Stacey while we were being dragged away. Meanwhile, unbeknownst to us, the Twittersphere was lighting up.

The crowd in front of SWSA was buzzing about Ben, while our family remained inside a magical Snow White bubble. During the next ride I suggested that maybe it was time for a break, and that I would take Ben to the restroom. Aside from the obvious fact that he probably needed it, it would also be good for him to have a few minutes completely alone inside a nice quiet stall in order to decompress a little. His mom readily agreed, and for the first and last time that evening we left the immediate premises of SWSA.

Meanwhile back in the Snow White line, talk was spreading about Ben and his history with the ride. I discovered this blog the next day:

> *Today the Disney community truly joined together to pay honor to this classic attraction that is leaving way too soon. While most would think people would be fighting over who would be the last to go, something much more magical happened. There was a boy present who has always considered Snow White's Scary Adventures to be his favorite attraction. He and his family have ridden over 2,000 times prior to this week and Disney has helped him this week hit 3,000 rides.*

> *At 7, he was accompanied by Snow White herself for one final ride. I stood near the exit and the look of pure happiness upon the boy's face brought tears to*

everyone's eyes. It was at that moment everyone
seemed to have a mutual understanding: he must be
the last rider on this attraction.
- excerpted from Brent Dodge's blog at
FromScreenToTheme.com

By a quarter to eight we were back at the ride and settling into a groove. Although the alternate entrance wasn't quite as backed up as it had been, Ben's mom and I basically started taking turns standing in line. While one was on the ride with Ben, the other would wait in line for the next go-around. We were up to around ride 3,460 when Ben's mom said that Ben could absolutely get to ride number 3,500 before the end of the night. I looked at my watch, did the math, and pointed out that it was just mathematically impossible. Impossible? Ha! Full steam ahead, and by God we'll make it! I never believed it for a moment, but it was something to keep us old folks engaged as Ben rapturously drank in ride after ride.

The evening became a blur, and throughout it we kept meeting interesting people. One was Kenneth Sundberg (a.k.a. KenNetti), author of the website Snow White's Adventures: The Tribute (http://www.kennetti.fi), who had flown all the way from Finland to witness the closing of the ride first-hand. Another was the guy wearing a "Save Snow White's Adventures!" t-shirt, who was thrilled to be able to say hello to Ben.

We met a mother with her two young autistic children, also looping through the alternate entrance at the same pace as us. At one point I noticed another mom with an autistic boy who was only a year or two younger than Ben. This boy's entire demeanor reminded me so much of Ben, the hand flapping, the huge smile, the big hugs. He was having a great night as well, and his mom was rightly proud.

On one ride while Ben and I were sitting in the second row of the mine cart, the guy in the front row turned around and introduced himself as Kevin Yee. He started to explain who he was, but I recognized the name immediately as I had often read his columns on MiceAge.com. He told me that he had taken several pictures from Ben's ride with Snow White, and he would be happy to send them to me.

Varsenik Wilson
@mansonrepublica
*I was lucky enough to have Ben in my mine cart for
my 33rd ride today. You can really see him light up
when he's on #SWSA.*

More rides, more people. As nine o'clock came and went we counted up to 3,475 rides while the clock counted down to the ride's closing. Ben was still going strong with no hint of tiring, as his normal bedtime flew past.

Meanwhile the crowd continued to be festive and celebratory. Among those coming to pay their final respects was a mother dressed impeccably as the Evil Queen, complete with a lovely red apple in her hand, along with her young daughter dressed as Snow White. They were real crowd pleasers.

Also present was my friend and fellow Snow White enthusiast, documentary filmmaker Robert Lughai (first name pronounced 'rowBEAR' with a French inflection). He had generously offered to film Ben's last night on the ride so that we would have some kind of keepsake to commemorate the event. Throughout the night, Robert continued filming Ben as much as possible without intruding or distracting, but as it got darker out and Robert had to start using his lights, it became yet another indication to the crowd that something big was going on with Ben. Periodically Stacey would check in to see that Ben was doing okay, and the other cast members performed like rock stars keeping everything rolling along.

Around 9:30pm we were delighted by the surprise appearance of Ben's grandfather. He works in Maintenance for the Magic Kingdom. I gathered he had decided to come in a little early for his shift that night so that he could see Ben. Not surprisingly, Ben was thrilled to see Grandpa the next time he came through the line. He was not quite so thrilled that he was willing to slow down his pace. By then Ben was up to 3,482 rides and he wasn't slowing down for anything.

I think it was somewhere around then that the Fantasyland courtyard was cleared in preparation for the Wishes fireworks show. The line for SWSA was rerouted to run back in front of the Seven Dwarfs Mine gift shop and along back by The Friar's Nook. I could no longer tell by looking just how long the line was, I only heard snippets of conversation from the crowd about how far back it stretched. And still the steady countdown to the end marched onward as Ben's ride count ratcheted up and up.

The fireworks started at 10pm; for those of us in front of SWSA it felt like they were all for us, a fitting pyrotechnic salute to an attraction that had served the Magic Kingdom proudly since opening day on October 1st, 1971. Normally Ben doesn't like the loud thundering of the fireworks' shells, but he was *in the zone* and not letting up.

Somewhere shortly after the fireworks I had a brief conversation with Stacey and mentioned that Ben was actually up to 3,490 rides. "It's crazy," I said, "but he just might make it. All you have to do is slow down the line!" I said it with a laugh, and I was by no means serious. The line had been capped at 10pm so that no further guests could join it, and I knew that it wouldn't be much longer before it was all over. There certainly wasn't a half hour's worth of people left waiting in the queue; Ben would finish his SWSA career somewhere in the low 3,490s.

And then suddenly, at 10:27pm, it was the moment of truth. The clock had run out. There were no overtimes remaining. We came off of ride number 3,492 to find that there was nobody else left in line. A crowd had gathered along the rope line to cheer on the last riders. Ben was led to the empty loading zone along with the rest of us. The last few guests cycled out of their mine carts and then along came a cart that was empty but for an orange traffic cone placed in the front seat to indicate that there were no other occupied carts behind it.

Mark Diba
@Dibadisney
Ben and his family are the last guests to ride
#SWSA I'm about to cry again

The final mine cart to run through Snow White's Scary Adventures during normal operating hours was occupied by Ben and his mother in the front row, Ben's grandfather in the second row, and then me in the back. As we were about to load into the cart, we stressed to Ben that this was it, this was the last time ever that he would go on his ride. With swirling emotions we all climbed in and the ride operator sent us off on the final ride. The crowd cheered as we rolled around the wishing well, and then we were past Snow White singing on the steps of the palace and through the doors into the dark.

The magic mirror intones his prophecy. The Evil Queen transforms into the Old Hag. The skeleton rots in his jail cell while the Old Hag douses her ruby red apple into the poison-filled cauldron; through some gates as the Huntsman shouts his warning to the princess; her startled figure suddenly appearing among the dark roots of the trees ahead. The Old Hag punting her little boat as the log-crocodiles growl, and then on through the dark forest filled with the hag's cackling while the trees reach in from every direction. Suddenly a light ahead, as we make a turn through the Friendly Forest and into the Cottage of the Seven Dwarfs. There they are, all lined up dancing and singing a silly song, while just around the corner Snow White accepts the Old Hag's poisoned apple. Then out the cottage doors on a mad chase to catch the witch, running through the jewel-encrusted mines as Bashful implores, "She's getting away... hurry!" And there atop the rocky crag stands the Old Hag herself, about to push a huge boulder down upon us before a surely-divinely-sent bolt of lightning ends her evil quest. And now, a ray of hope — there is the young and handsome Prince Charming, awakening the princess with Love's First Kiss. The music swells, the forest fills with light, and the prince leads Snow White away along a beautiful stone bridge towards his castle shining in the distance while the dwarfs wave a final farewell. Just above the last door is Dopey, with his big silly grin and waggling ears, waving goodbye for the very last time.

Amy Patricia
@AliceHermione
Standing ovation for last rider of #swsa brought
tears to my eyes. Good night sweet princess

We exited the ride to thunderous applause. I was satisfied that the old girl had received a fitting fare-thee-well. Sure, Ben had missed a huge milestone number by only seven rides, but honestly 3,493 felt pretty dang good. And terribly sad.

But the amazing thing was, the night wasn't over. Stacey still had one more trick up her sleeve.

The crowd was still cheering as Stacey led our group away from Snow White's Scary Adventures following the official last ride. Just like a few hours earlier, we were taken to a spot in front of The Friar's Nook in order to wait. We watched as Disney security helped guide the remaining guests out of Fantasyland. As the park quickly emptied out, we learned that Stacy had another gift for Ben, a photo CD with more than 80 pictures taken during Snow White's visit with Ben, along with four prints of some of the best shots. Ben particularly liked the one from inside the ride with Snow White. I particularly liked the one showing Ben laughing and happy.

Ben describes his day in precisely 1,000 words

While we waited, Ben's grandpa said his goodbyes and left for work. Our remaining group consisted of Ben, Sara, videographer Robert Lughai, Finnish Snow White aficionado Kenneth Sundberg, and me. After a few minutes Stacey came back and said that the park guests were all clear, and that we could go back and finish the rides to get Ben up to 3,500. What? We were stunned and had to take that in for a second. Walt Disney World was keeping the ride open for an additional 25 minutes *exclusively for Ben*. It was already nearing 11pm, and I have to imagine that workers were standing by to begin decommissioning the ride and putting up the construction walls that had to be in place before park opening the next day, but here they were letting my family and friends back on the ride for no other reason than to finish with a milestone number.

That's not "above and beyond", it's just a whole new dimension of amazing.

The atmosphere as the five of us loaded into the mine cart was completely different from earlier. Before it had been a huge event with hundreds of strangers. Now it had become an intimate affair shared among just a handful of trusted compatriots.

We had the entire ride to ourselves, and our interactions became downright surreal. Ben was still giddy with joy. With no other guests to bother we felt free to have full-voiced conversations throughout the ride pointing out little detail bits that we loved. On one of the early laps, Sara mentioned that she had always wanted to touch the wishing well but had never tried because the cast member operating the ride would notice and she didn't want to get kicked out of the park. So of course on the next lap I looked her straight in the eyes and reached out to touch the well as we spun around. She couldn't reach it all from her seat, and so on the next go-around she traded places and finally her wish was fulfilled.

I think it was after the second lap, at ride number 3,495, that we realized that we didn't need to be lugging around all of our backpacks and such. (Spending hours in the park with a special needs child requires a variety of supplies and I had been lugging around that backpack all night). With no other guests to worry about, we just piled up our belongings next to the unload station and carried on. After each lap we would have to exit the cart, and then walk around to get back into the very same cart again. During each transition the cast members would count out the next ride number, like the slowest New Year's Eve countdown ever.

Around the 3,498th ride Sara looked at me and said, "I think he should go on the last ride all by himself."

My heart nearly stopped at such a notion.

In eighteen years, Benjamin had never been truly alone. Sure, he might be alone in another room in the house — places that were absolutely safe and quickly accessible by a guardian if anything should happen. But he had never, ever been somewhere completely unsupervised, completely unobserved and unobservable. I almost said "no" immediately, but in my heart I realized that his mother was right. Ben was legally an adult. He had a lap bar to prevent him from exiting the ride vehicle. He would be fine. Almost certainly. If ever there was an opportunity to let him go on a ride on his own, this was it. It was a way to make the final ride really and truly special. By the 3,499th ride we were in agreement, although my stomach was still twisting in knots at the idea.

And then, it was the moment of truth. We all exited the cart. Ken stood off at a respectable distance, allowing us to have this moment as a family. Robert collected his camera and set up to film Ben's last ride. We led Ben over to the loading zone, gave him a big hug, and then told him to go ahead. He looked a little confused at first and then smiled in disbelief. With his iPod in one hand, a single earbud in his left ear, and with his camera in the other hand he embarked on the very last ride. We waved and blew him kisses as he rounded the wishing well, and then he was through the doors and completely gone.

I turned to Stacey and said, "There are cameras in there, right? There's somebody in a security room somewhere that can see everything that is happening?"

"Nope!" she replied cheerfully, "but there are intrusion mats everywhere. In any case the lap bar will keep him in the cart." I knew about the intrusion mats, which are pressure-sensitive rubber rectangles placed on the floor in strategic locations that will halt the ride if anyone steps on them. Their presence, though, did not provide me any peace of mind.

I looked at my watch, and then looked at the exit doors. Empty cart after empty cart paraded by. I had visions of those doors opening to a cart vacant but for an iPod and a camera perched on the front seat. The headlines the next day would read "Autistic Boy Disappears from Disney Ride". I imagined a vignette several decades in the future, a grizzled old coot of a maintenance worker saying in hushed tones to a new employee, "...and to this day you can hear his ghost moaning in this building, mourning the loss of his favorite ride..."

Surely it had been three minutes by now, and still Ben had yet to appear. I realized that I was holding my breath, as I noticed abstractly that Robert had set up his camera shot to get the perfect view of Ben's exit. Finally, after what seemed like hours, those doors swung open and there was my happy young man still clutching his iPod and his camera. We all let out a cheer as the mine cart rolled to a halt, and then Benjamin got big hugs all around.

And that is how it was that Benjamin's actual last ride was a huge milestone. Not because of the big round number, and not because he was the last guest to ever go on the ride, but because that final ride was the first step on a terrifying and exhilarating new adventure. All alone in that mine cart, Benjamin took his first giant step towards independence. Three minutes alone on a dark ride may seem like a small thing, but for our family it was a tremendously magnificent feat. Of everything else that happened on that remarkable night, that is the thing that will be etched into my memory forever.

After Ben completed his final ride on Snow White's Scary Adventures, we gave our heartfelt thanks to all of the remaining cast members. Then we were escorted out of Fantasyland so that the maintenance workers could get on with the task of erecting the construction walls. Ken thanked us for allowing him to share in the experience of those last half-dozen rides. Then he and Robert left for their respective lodgings for the night. Even though it was well past eleven, Ben was still buzzing from the whole experience and didn't show any signs of winding down. We crossed under the castle and then down through the hub, merging with the last of the lingering crowd on Main Street.

By the time we exited the park the monorail was already shut down for the night. We had to wait in line for a ferry boat instead. Ben was starting to agitate about Tinkerbell, so I dug out the Tink ornament that we had purchased at the start of the evening. That placated him at least for a while, but it was clear that he was on the edge of tipping over from happy to tired and cranky. I dearly hoped we would manage to get him all the way to the car before that particular time bomb detonated. Fortunately, the boat came quickly and before long we were walking through the Ticket and Transportation Center en route to the car. Ben stopped to take a photo of a Tinkerbell window decoration, which was when I thought to take a glance at his camera to see if he actually took any pictures during that last solo ride. As a matter of fact, he did capture a shot of his absolute favorite moment of the ride — Bashful in the mine crying, "She's getting away, hurry!"

The very last photo taken by any guest on Snow White's Scary Adventures

Arriving at the car without incident, I gave Ben his nighttime meds and started the drive home. Usually in the car he would listen to his iPod (almost exclusively Disney soundtracks) but for this occasion I went ahead and let him listen to the Snow White soundtrack on the car stereo. He would usually play the same track, or part of a track, over and over again, which could get a little trying. That night I was fine with it. For most of the drive he kept listening to the crescendo of music from the scene where the Huntsman warns Snow White to run away, followed by her terrified dash through the forest. It starts quietly, builds slowly, and then comes to a crashing climax. I heard that same track over and over again for about fifteen minutes, then as we were nearing home, he started skipping ahead through the album.

Now this, you are going to think, is something I made up for dramatic license. I swear to you it is not the case. Anyone who knows me will tell you I just don't know how to make anything up and that I am a terrible liar. I simply could not have dreamed up this ending to the drive if I had tried.

Ben very specifically and deliberately skipped ahead to track number 24, "Love's First Kiss". It is from the last scene of the movie, where the dwarfs are gathered around Snow White's glass coffin mourning her death until Prince Charming arrives to break the spell. Ben started the track when we were still about two miles from home; as we entered our housing complex it was reaching its triumphant ending. I pulled into the driveway just as the final fanfare ended, where the movie would fade out after the final caption of "The End".

It was just the perfect serendipitous touch to cap off an amazing day.

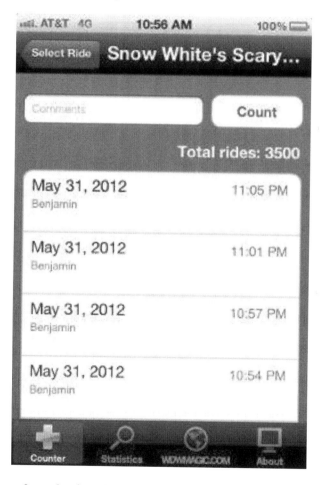

Screenshot from the RideCounter app I used to keep count

Chapter 18

The Aftermath

Twelve days after the closing of Snow White's Scary Adventures, enough time had passed that we figured we should take Ben to the park, let him see with his own eyes that the ride is really gone. The weather in Central Florida had been miserable for most of the week, with nice enough mornings but storms sweeping through by mid-afternoon. I'm a Seattle boy, born and raised, so rain doesn't bother me much. As for Ben, I sometimes wonder if he even notices something as trivial as the weather.

That Thursday had been the last day of the school year; Ben was at my house all day Friday while I worked in my home office. By the time I had enough done that I could get away from work, the weather was too miserable even for a soggy-friendly Washingtonian like me. Ben had been asking to "take a tram" all that day. I promised him that on Saturday we would go.

By late Saturday morning Ben was nagging me constantly — "Daddy... I want... take-a-tram! Go see... Tinkerbell..."

We loaded up our gear and headed out. It wasn't raining yet, but the sky was certainly making threatening overtures by the time we arrived at the

Zurg parking lot and started walking in to the Ticket and Transportation Center. So far, Ben had not mentioned Snow White at all. Everything was "take-a-tram", "Tinkerbell", and "Fantasia". I was not surprised when he led me to the resort monorail instead of the express to the Magic Kingdom. We rode around to the Contemporary Hotel to visit the Fantasia store. Ben spent a fair amount of time taking pictures of the enchanted brooms, as well as a few pins and various other merchandise. Then, he did something brand new, leading me out the back of the hotel and over to the pool area.

We had lived in Central Florida for almost a decade, and had been to Disney more times than I can count, but I had never even *seen* the pool area of the Contemporary. It just had never come up. But Ben, he wanted to go check it out and take a few pictures. Then, of course, he wanted to go for a swim. I had to talk him out of that as gently as possible. It helped that a thunderstorm started rolling in just then, causing the pool area to be closed and evacuated. (Pro tip: The last place to be when there is lightning is standing in a swimming pool.)

As we walked away from the pool, Ben turned to me and finally said the words I was dreading: "More Snow White, please!"

The drizzle slowly increased to a steady rainfall as we walked the pathway from the Contemporary to the Magic Kingdom. For the entire walk I reminded Ben that Snow White was closed, all gone. We could go see Pooh ... Tomorrowland (Ben short-code for the Tomorrowland Transit Authority) ... Pirates ... Still Ben looked up at me with a slight desperation in his eyes and repeated "More Snow White, please!"

We were thoroughly sodden by the time we went through the turnstiles at the entrance to the Magic Kingdom. Sara met us at the park on the theory that it would be best if we were both there with him the first time he came face-to-face with the construction walls. He walked up Main Street with a determined gait, first walking through the Main Street Confectionery but hardly giving anything a glance, and then he was up into the hub and angling to the right towards Cosmic Ray's. From there he took a sharp left up the pathway past the Wishing Well, and in moments we were in Fantasyland.

As usual he went right into the gift shop adjacent to SWSA. That is where he encountered the first blow to his system. The doorway that he would normally exit through, which would lead him to the alternate entrance to SWSA, was closed and barred. He stopped dead in his tracks and tilted his head as he considered this oddity. Then he cut out the side door to go around. That is where he came full face with the giant blue wall that had been erected around his favorite place in the world.

He glanced up: I saw him notice that even the name of the ride was gone from the still-visible structure above the walls. He walked the entire length of the wall, all the way to the Seven Dwarfs Mine shop; then he followed the wall around into the dim back corner where the featureless blue barrier came to an end. He searched for a door there but to no avail. All the while his mother and I explained to him gently that Snow White was closed, that it was all gone. He took his mother's hand and then trudged back along the wall in the drizzling rain, still searching for a way in.

The good news was that he did not have a meltdown. I was genuinely worried that he would get upset and frustrated when he discovered his ride was really gone. He stayed surprisingly calm. He went back to the gift shop and looked at the closed door a little longer, and for just a moment he looked like he was going to tip over the edge. Then he took out his camera and focused on a tiny plush Sorcerer Mickey doll instead and took its picture. A few more snaps, and then, in a dejected whisper he said, "Monorail."

Sara took to calling that spot The Graveyard Of Snow White's Scary Adventures (jokingly referred to as The Graveyard). I wholeheartedly agreed with that description. A week or so later, on Ben's second visit back, he again went straight to The Graveyard and seemed generally depressed about it.

Sara and Ben

In order to distract him and show him some of the new things in the park, I took him over to the new Dumbo location, and we actually took a spin around. One of the cast members working the ride was a regular from Snow White, and he gave Ben a big high five and welcomed him to the new ride. For Ben's part, he was pretty ambivalent about the whole thing. He seemed like he was just humoring me by going on the ride; he certainly did not seem to get any enjoyment out of it. As soon as it was over he dragged me back over to The Graveyard for another check to see if maybe Disney had changed their minds in the previous thirty minutes. Then he took me right to the Monorail to get out.

Several weeks passed before visit number three, before Ben actually *asked* once again to go "take a tram". Walking into the park he gave me a hopeful look and said, "Go see… Snow White?" It broke my heart to have to tell him yet again that the ride was gone forever. The visit played out much like the previous two, with a sad trek to The Graveyard and several minutes spent gazing longingly at the construction walls. I offered almost every other ride in the park, but he wasn't buying. I did at least get him to take a side trip and go visit the Princesses at the meet and greet, down on Main Street. He was extremely patient waiting in the line, and he seemed genuinely thrilled to visit with both Cinderella and Belle. He was even very polite to Rapunzel, although he had no idea who she was. In the end he walked out of the park smiling and happy, so that was nice.

His next visit post-SWSA was with his mom, and it turned out to be a great visit. Yes, he still walked by

The Graveyard, but he also went on several rides like the Tomorrowland Transit Authority, Haunted Mansion, and Pirates of the Caribbean. As a matter of fact, he went on Haunted Mansion twice and was laughing and talking the whole time they were in line. Sara also took him over to the construction walls with the artwork for the new Seven Dwarfs Mine Ride. In her own words:

> "On our way out, I walked him over to the big mural on the construction wall, showing what the new ride will look like. I talked him through what we were looking at, and he repeated the phrase, 'Mine car' & touched parts of the picture. The description of the ride says that it's a 'musical adventure' and that the ride will end with your mine car 'arriving at the cottage, where Snow White is waiting to welcome you home.' He liked the sound of that."

A few months later, in mid-October, I heard that the New Fantasyland area was soft open (an industry term meaning the area was open and operating on a limited basis, although not appearing on the official park maps yet). The soft opening included the new Journey of the Little Mermaid ride. With any luck, our months of waiting were over and Ben would discover a new favorite ride.

We arrived at the park, Ben made a brief side trip through the shops on Main Street, and then we were headed back to Fantasyland. My first pleasant surprise as we walked into the Carrousel courtyard was to see that the last of the construction barriers had come down from around the new castle walls that had been erected to visually separate Old Fantasyland from New Fantasyland. For the first time, in seemingly forever, the core of Fantasyland was wide open and free of construction. It looked spectacular. We walked through the stone arches into the new Enchanted Forest and Ben began to get a little bit interested.

As we worked our way past Belle's village, over into the domain of Prince Eric, we were disappointed to find that Journey of the Little Mermaid was currently down for some kind of repairs or adjustments. Of course Ben had no idea what he was missing, and so he was perfectly happy to let me take him to the new Ariel's Grotto where he got to sit down and visit with Ariel herself.

Once we finished with Ariel, we strolled over to Tomorrowland for a leisurely ride on the Tomorrowland Transit Authority. By the time we completed that, nearly an hour had passed so we meandered back over to New Fantasyland. As we approached the entrance to Journey of the Little Mermaid, I could see that guests were entering the queue and the ride was apparently back up and running. The moment of truth at last!

Ben was very patient as I led him through the line. He liked all of the water features and thought some of the sculptures were cool, but he was completely clueless as to what was about to happen. We came around the turn, and he saw for the very first time the huge mural on the wall behind the loading station. The mural is a massive panoramic painting of the ocean shore with Prince Eric's castle on the left and the Little Mermaid herself perched on a rock in the bay gazing across the water to Prince Eric's ship. A tiny smile crept onto Ben's face, as he seemed to tumble to what he was actually visiting. Quickly enough we were loaded into our clamshell ride vehicle, and we drifted past Scuttle giving his intro spiel.

At the next show area Ben suddenly grew a huge smile becoming 100% engaged in the ride. Ariel was singing "Part of Your World", and Ben was transfixed. For the next 5 1/2 minutes he took it all in with an omnipresent smile, along with several instances of outright laughter. Song after song floated by and Ben was engrossed in every single detail. Here was the evil Sea Witch tempting Ariel with her enchantment to make the Little Mermaid a human. There was the huge room with all of the singing and dancing sea life while Sebastian the Crab sang "Under the Sea"; another section featured the romantic boat ride with Ariel and Prince Eric gazing lovingly at each other while Sebastian crooned "Kiss the Girl". Finally the ride came to an end and with some reluctance we exited the building. Outside I asked Ben what he thought and he had one very simple response:

"Ride!"

He took me by the hand and led me straight back to the ride entrance for a second trip. For the first time in over four months I finally felt like he had his park back. It might not truly be his Happy Place, but in a lot of ways I think Journey of the Little Mermaid offers a very welcome evolution. First of all, the ride itself is twice as long as Snow White's Scary Adventures; and secondly, the nature of the entrance and exit means that it is impossible for him to simply do laps on the ride. It was possible to do 3 laps around Snow White's Scary Adventures in under ten minutes, it would take the better part of a half hour to accomplish the same thing on Journey of the Little Mermaid in even the best of crowd conditions. Because of that, it would be very difficult for the new ride to become as obsessive as his old one. He can go and enjoy it, maybe even twice in a row, but with enough space between rides to help prevent the mental feedback loop that keeps him so strongly attached.

All total we went on Journey of the Little Mermaid four times that day over the course of several hours. Ben seemed completely happy and satiated with that amount. I think we spent perhaps four hours in the park, all of which he thoroughly enjoyed. It was a perfect day in the Magic Kingdom, and a huge relief.

Of course, Ben being Ben, he is not *entirely* satisfied with the opening of Journey of the Little Mermaid. No, he has made a point of taking us over to the artwork on the last major construction wall in the New Fantasyland expansion. It is the one that depicts the new Seven Dwarf's Mine Cart ride. He gets a twinkle in his eye, points at the picture, and says, "Mine cart!" So, although the long wait for the Little Mermaid is finally over, apparently now the clock is ticking impatiently as we count down to 2014....

Epilogue

During the week after the closing of Snow White's Scary Adventures, I wrote a song for and about my son. It encapsulates all of my feelings about the entire Snow White experience, distilled down to just a few minutes. I am not a professional musician by any means, but I have been singing since I was a teenager and have played guitar on and off since then as well. When I played it for Ben he seemed to enjoy it, and I hope that you would enjoy it as well. The lyrics are reproduced below, and information about the song itself is available at Shmoolok.com where I blog about Ben and autism.

Benjamin's Lullaby (a.k.a. All Is Well)

It was a silly old fairytale ride
And for forty long years they ran it with pride
There were dwarfs and a princess inside
Just three minutes long
Overflowing with song
And although it was not the most popular ride
The children all loved it so well

The lap bar goes down as the mine cart rolls on
By the wishing well a princess is singing her song
There's a scary old witch
And a dark gloomy forest as well
In their cottage the dwarfs have a silly good time
And a handsome young prince breaks the spell
All is well

Now Ben wasn't like other kids
His autism left him without any friends
He spent his time trapped in his head
And although often heard
He'd never spoken a word
But the very first time he stepped into that park
Ben was cast under a spell

The lap bar goes down as the mine cart rolls on
By the wishing well a princess is singing her song
There's a scary old witch
And a dark gloomy forest as well
In their cottage the dwarfs have a silly good time
And a handsome young prince breaks the spell
All is well

As he rode and he rode
We saw his language explode
He went time and again
And began to make friends
His senses were thrumming
And we saw him coming
Alive

It was ten years he went on that ride
He grew three feet taller
And his problems grew smaller
His progress, it filled me with pride
Still a long way to go
But he'll make it, I know

And then came the day
That his ride went away
And he'll never go on it again

The lap bar goes down as the mine cart rolls on
By the wishing well a princess is singing her song
There's a scary old witch
And a dark gloomy forest as well
In their cottage the dwarfs have a silly good time
And a handsome young prince breaks the spell
All is well

And it's exactly three thousand five hundred times
That Ben was cast under that spell
All is well

Benjamin's Lullaby

Ron Miles is the proud father of an autistic son, a software architect, and a musician. Born and raised in the Pacific Northwest, Ron moved (along with his ex-wife, son, and then-fiancée) to Central Florida in the summer of 2003 in order to use Walt Disney World as a giant therapy session for his son. He blogs about his son and other autism-related issues at www.shmoolok.com. He also runs a website dedicated to post-apocalyptic fiction at www.JamesAxler.com, as well at least a dozen other websites. In his day job he works from a home office and writes the software that drives the Conferences & Events department of a luxury travel company. He dreams of the day when he will finally be able to have a real conversation his son, if only to find out what his son has really been thinking about all these years.

www.shmoolok.com

Made in the USA
Lexington, KY
27 August 2013